Special Events Contingency Planning

Job Aids Manual

March 2005

 FEMA

TABLE OF CONTENTS

TABLE OF CONTENTS (CONTINUED)

TABLE OF CONTENTS (CONTINUED)

ACKNOWLEDGEMENTS

The following agencies are gratefully acknowledged for their input to this manual:

Federal Emergency Management Agency

FEMA National Fire Academy

Virginia Department of Health

New York State Police

City of Keene Police Department, New Hampshire

Sarasota Fire Department, Florida

Washington, DC Fire and EMS Department

Miami-Dade Office of Emergency Management, Fire-Rescue Department, Florida

Cabin John Park Volunteer Fire Department, Maryland

Marion County Emergency Management, Indiana

Massachusetts Emergency Management Agency

Weber County Emergency Management, Utah

Washington D.C. Office of Emergency Preparedness

Utah Division of Comprehensive Emergency Management

Columbia South Carolina Public Works

American Public Works Association

Acknowledgement is also made of the manual, *Safe and Healthy Mass Gatherings: A Health, Medical and Safety Planning Manual for Public Events*, prepared by Emergency Management Australia, and of the paper, *Emergency Preparedness Guidelines for Mass, Crowd-Intensive Events*, prepared for Emergency Preparedness Canada by James A. Hanna, M. SC.

INTRODUCTION

PREFACE

The purpose of this manual is the prevention of injury, suffering, or death that may occur as a result of poor planning or preventable incidents at public events.

This manual is intended to provide guidance for the management of risks associated with conducting events that involve mass gatherings of people and assist planners and organizers in making such events safe and successful.

Details of the development of the manual and other related matters are noted in the Background section of the Introduction. The manual was sponsored, edited, and published by the Department of Homeland Security (DHS)/Federal Emergency Management Agency (FEMA).

FEMA has prepared this manual for use by anyone planning or conducting a special event or mass gathering. This manual is intended to enable its users to ensure that adequate measures and systems are in place to prevent, reduce, and provide care for injuries, illness, and suffering that may occur.

Many people, in addition to health personnel, contribute significantly to the success of a public event. Therefore, FEMA anticipates that this manual will be distributed to event promoters, managers, public and private organizations, emergency service personnel, government bodies, and any individual or organization that contributes to the planning of events. Wide distribution is encouraged, providing that individuals understand that the detailed contents of the manual are directed principally at managing the health and safety aspects of the event for all participants, officials, and spectators.

The manual is not intended to override any existing legislation or local emergency management procedures. Further, it does not seek to address the preparation of emergency response plans, but rather identifies the elements that should be considered by those responsible for planning and conducting events that attract large numbers of people.

Local governments and emergency services should be approached for more detailed advice on other aspects of planning and for the necessary permits and licenses required.

BACKGROUND

Throughout the United States, at any given time of year, there are festivals, concerts, fairs, sporting events, and many other large and small events that gather or have the potential to gather large crowds. Under normal conditions, these events go on with few or no problems. When something goes wrong, however, either as a result of a natural hazard or a man-made hazard, then local emergency management becomes involved. These mass gatherings are also potential targets for terrorists.

Multiple deaths and injuries at large public events have occurred consistently and over a wide spectrum of countries and types of events. Certain highly competitive sports events, particularly soccer, and rock concerts and festivals tend to produce spectator-generated incidents, while air shows and auto races tend to produce more participant-generated occurrences.

In some instances, advanced assessment of, and planning for, these events failed to occur, or when they did, they failed to identify the potential for disaster, or mitigating or coping strategies for a major incident.

With this in mind, FEMA conducted a focus group workshop during which participants discussed real pre-event planning problems for an upcoming event. The workshop focused on a number of major areas, which, either singularly or collectively, have intensified the problems inherent in mass crowd-intensive events. These issues included such aspects as physical layouts, spectator management, public safety, public health, and medical care.

The workshop was not geared toward large, often national events (i.e., Incidents of National Significance, National Special Security Events, though the planning principles still apply), but toward the more "routine" special events that communities host, such as parades, fairs, concerts, and air shows.

The participants focused on the impact that an event, a non-routine activity, would have on a community's resources. They placed emphasis not on the total number of people attending, but rather on the community's ability to respond to the exceptional demands that the activity would place on response services.

The purpose of having a pre-event plan in place is to reduce response times and better enable agencies to improvise because they have discussed contingencies beforehand. A pre-event plan defines roles and responsibilities in advance and creates ownership of potential problems for agencies that are involved in the process.

On February 28, 2003, the President issued Homeland Security Presidential Directive (HSPD)–5, *Management of Domestic Incidents*, which directs the Secretary of Homeland Security to develop and administer a National Incident Management System (NIMS). This system provides a consistent nationwide template to enable Federal, State, local, and tribal governments and private-sector and non-governmental organizations to work together effectively and efficiently to prepare for, prevent, respond to, and recover from domestic incidents, regardless of cause, size, or complexity, including acts of catastrophic terrorism.

BACKGROUND (CONTINUED)

The NIMS provides a set of standardized organizational structures—such as the Incident Command System (ICS), multi-agency coordination systems, and public information systems—as well as requirements for processes, procedures, and systems designed to improve interoperability among jurisdictions and disciplines in various areas, to include: training; resource management; personnel qualification and certification; equipment certification; communications and information management; technology support; and continuous system improvement. ICS should be used in responding to an incident during a special event.

This manual is designed for a wide audience, encompassing the range of personnel with a role to play in the development of a special event plan. Participants include those who have a general awareness of their own roles but do not have a previous detailed or extensive knowledge of special event planning. For example, the audience might include relatively new emergency managers, personnel from emergency operations organizations such as police, fire, medical services, and public works, and representatives from other community organizations—both public and private—for whom special event planning is not a regular responsibility.

SCOPE

The suggested guidelines in this manual have been developed from a number of sources, and most are applicable to a wide range of mass public gatherings. These sources focused on youth audiences attending large rock concerts and competitive sporting events because of the difficulties and major incidents historically associated with such events. Many of the guidelines derived from such experiences are applicable to a broad range of other events that present their own challenges.

Certain types of events have an inherent capacity for special management problems. While the general guidance given in this document remains applicable to these events, additional guidance is given for high-risk events in Chapter 4: Additional Planning Considerations for Specific Events.

In certain situations, such as visits by high-profile political figures or controversial activists, intensive security arrangements are necessary. Such procedures are outside the scope of this manual, and it would be inappropriate and counterproductive to provide details herein, given the wide and unrestricted distribution of this document. When such events occur, event planners must create liaison between emergency service personnel, health professionals, and appropriate security personnel to ensure that they address health, safety and security issues for the event.

SYNOPSIS

This manual covers a number of major areas, which either singularly of collectively, have historically exacerbated the problems inherent in mass crowd-intensive events. These areas include such aspects as physical layouts (including site, structures, and access), spectator management (including crowd organization, flow, and ingress/egress control), and public safety (including security, public health, and medical care).

Historically, advance assessment of and planning for an event failed to occur, or when they did, they failed to identify the potential for disaster or mitigating or coping strategies in the event of a major incident.

Experience has proven that certain high-risk events, such as auto races and air shows, require particular planning in addition to the more generally applicable guidelines. This manual provides guidance for the particular planning of these high-risk events, as well as guidance to plan for terrorist and criminal activities.

FEMA recognizes that no two events or situations are identical. While this document provides an approach to planning for and coping with special events, it does not provide guidelines that are universally applicable or without need of modification to the specifics of a particular event.

CHAPTER OVERVIEWS

Chapter 1 contains information concerning selection of the planning team, ordinances, regulations, and laws, and information concerning selecting a site for the event.

Chapter 2 concerns the event's operational considerations.

Chapter 3 gives a basic overview of the NIMS Incident Command System and how to use ICS both in the planning stage and when an incident occurs.

Chapter 4 discusses some of the considerations when hosting a specialty event that may be high risk.

Chapter 5 explains the demobilization process and the importance of an After-Action Report.

Appendix A contains job aids to assist in the planning process.

Appendix B contains references and a bibliography.

Appendix C contains a glossary of terms.

CHAPTER 1: PRE-EVENT PLANNING

INTRODUCTION

Planning any event is difficult. Planning for the potential risks and hazards associated with an event is even more difficult but essential to the event's success. If you want those who attend an event to have positive memories of it, you need to keep several things in mind. This chapter covers the issues that you should address in the very early stages of planning or even when you are discussing promoting or sponsoring such an event. Before you schedule the event, you should consider the scope of the event or mass gathering, the risks to spectators and participants, community impact, and the emergency support required (personnel and logistics). You should also identify the lead agency and members of the planning team.

DEFINITION OF SPECIAL EVENT AND MASS GATHERING

What does or does not constitute a special event or mass gathering is difficult to determine. Instead, guidelines may be used to define it.

A focus group discussing special events and mass gatherings has identified a special event as:

> **a non-routine activity within a community that brings together a large number of people. Emphasis is not placed on the total number of people attending but rather the impact on the community's ability to respond to a large-scale emergency or disaster or the exceptional demands that the activity places on response services. A community's special event requires additional planning, preparedness, and mitigation efforts of local emergency response and public safety agencies.**

The focus group then defined a mass gathering as a subset of a special event. Mass gatherings are usually found at special events that attract large numbers of spectators or participants. Both special events and mass gatherings require the kind of additional planning identified in the previous quote. For example, an amusement park that attracts a large number of people is not considered a special event because large crowds are expected. A mass gathering does not imply that the event is a special event. Failure to prepare for all contingencies can lead to disastrous consequences.

This manual is not intended to offer preparation planning for large national events, but for the more traditional community events, such as parades, fairs, concerts, air shows, and festivals. Both types of events require the same kind of careful planning, however.

The title of this manual is **<u>Special Events Contingency Planning</u>**. What do we mean by contingency planning and where do we start? What distinguishes this level of planning from traditional public safety planning?

DEFINITION OF SPECIAL EVENT AND MASS GATHERING (CONTINUED)

The first concern with contingency planning is to identify times when the event may place strains on the existing public safety agencies. Even in the earliest stages of planning, you should begin also to make contingency plans. These plans should consider licensing and regulations, emergency response issues, identifying persons responsible for particular types of hazards and risks, resources and expenses, and jurisdictions. Planning ahead reduces stress for organizers and promoters during the event, if an incident occurs that requires public agencies to work together.

During the initial planning stages, each agency should review resources to ensure that all necessary equipment is available. If the agencies determine that any additional equipment is needed, then they may acquire the equipment or supplies and be ready for the event. One way for communities to acquire equipment is to work together or pool equipment.

One way in which agencies work together is by adopting a program known as local mutual aid. This program allows neighboring communities to pool resources and share liability for damages or loss of equipment. If one community needs a particular piece of equipment, it may borrow it from a neighboring community. The equipment will become an asset of the borrowing community and will be covered under their insurance until it is released and returns to its home organization. It is important that those involved in planning the event know the agreements established between neighboring communities and the assets that are available to assist in responding to any unforeseen incidents. These agreements may all already be established and included as a part of the local emergency operations plan.

PLANNING MEETINGS FOR SPECIAL EVENTS/MASS GATHERINGS

PLANNING TEAM IDENTIFICATION

In general, planning a special event or mass gathering should begin well in advance of the event. One of the first steps in planning an event is to bring together those who are hosting the event with those who are responsible for the public safety within the community. A multidisciplinary planning team or committee should be composed of the promoter or sponsor and any agency that holds a functional stake in the event (e.g., emergency management, law enforcement, fire and rescue, public works/utilities, public health, etc.). With all of these agencies present, there is an obvious risk of confusion in matters of leadership. The nature of this risk is discussed in Chapter 3: Incident Command and Control. Thus, the lead agency should be identified early in the planning process. In some communities, the lead agency for public safety planning is the emergency management agency. Consequently, the emergency management agency should typically lead the way in coordinating the event planning effort.

Some communities already have planning protocols or systems in place. If your community has an existing plan that has already proved successful, do not start from scratch; simply change or modify the plan where needed. The ICS is a management system that is frequently used to manage large events effectively. As such, event planners should consider using ICS throughout the planning process. It seems logical that the Incident Commander should be a representative of the lead agency. It also seems logical that this representative should lead the planning team or committee.

PLANNING TEAM IDENTIFICATION (CONTINUED)

All involved agencies need to participate on this planning team from the outset to ensure a successful and safe event. At its initial meeting, the planning team should develop its mission and objectives, and determine the necessary components of the public safety plan. For example, what elements are within the realm of the promoter and what are within the realm of the public safety agencies? The planning team should also develop its structure using ICS as a model (that is, Sections, Branches, Divisions, and Groups, as needed). Chapter 3 will discuss ICS in greater detail. Additionally, the planning team should consider the promoter's or sponsoring organization's purpose and experience, potential event-related risks (including crowd control, staffing, food and shelter, parking, transportation, medical facilities), previous event concerns, relevant local concerns, weather, and community impact.

THE PLANNING PROCESS

TEAM APPROACH

Special event contingency plan development should be the joint effort of a planning team—a group of people who represent a cross-section of the organizations that are involved in the emergency response effort. Although each jurisdiction's team will vary somewhat, the Emergency Manager usually serves as the team's planning coordinator. Team members may include representatives of the groups listed below:

- Office of the Chief Executive.
- Promoter/Sponsor.
- Emergency services agencies (law enforcement, fire/rescue, emergency medical services, public health and safety, and others).
- Planning agencies and individuals (for example, community development, city planning commissions, and hazard mitigation planner).
- Local Emergency Planning Committees (LEPCs), for hazardous materials information.
- Public works agencies and utility companies.
- Social service agencies and volunteer organizations (including the American Red Cross and Salvation Army).
- Medical community representatives (for example, area hospitals, EMS agencies, medical examiner, coroner, mortician).
- Key education personnel (including administrators).
- Communications representatives (Public Information Officer (PIO), local media, radio/CB groups, and others).
- Aviation and coastal authorities (including State aviation authority, other air support representatives, port authorities, U.S. Coast Guard station).
- Chief Financial Officer (CFO), auditor, and heads of any centralized procurement and resource support agencies.
- The jurisdiction's legal counsel.
- Industrial and military installations in the area.
- Labor and professional organizations.
- Animal care and control organizations.
- Emergency Managers and agency representatives from neighboring jurisdictions, to coordinate mutual aid needs.

TEAM APPROACH (CONTINUED)

- State and/or Federal representatives, as appropriate.
- Representatives of private-sector organizations, as necessary.

A team approach to planning offers many advantages, including:

A Sense of Ownership – The plan is more likely to be used and followed if the tasked organizations have a sense that the plan is "theirs."

Greater Resources – More knowledge and expertise are brought to bear on the planning effort when more people are involved.

Cooperative Relationships – Closer professional relationships that are developed during the planning process should translate into better cooperation and coordination in emergencies.

STATE AND FEDERAL ROLES IN TERRORISM INCIDENT PREVENTION

An integrated approach among the local, State, and Federal Government provides for a logical clearinghouse for intelligence on the movement and activities of terrorist groups and the collection, interpretation, and dissemination of that information to the proper enforcement agencies. Effective planning and intelligence gathering can lessen the likelihood of a surprise emergency incident, which, improperly handled, can make or break a department and its administrators at all levels of government. Descriptive intelligence with predictive interpretation that forecasts the probability of the threat and the target can enhance operational readiness in training, equipping, and practicing to respond to emergency incidents. In gathering intelligence, law enforcement agencies must consider threat assessment, as a minimum measure. Planners must have appropriate contacts and phone numbers at hand before the event.

State law enforcement agencies should take the lead in pre-incident threat forecasting and planning. Roles and responsibilities of the various stakeholding agencies for the event need to be determined and an incident chain of command put in place, so that, if a terrorist threat materializes, confusion and duplication of response can be diminished.

PRE-EVENT PLANNING MATRIX

At subsequent meetings, the planning team should identify all of the major functions and responsibilities required by the event and assign appropriate agencies to manage each function or responsibility. Because responsibilities vary from jurisdiction to jurisdiction, it is most effective to assign responsibilities consistently to avoid duplication and promote efficient response to problems that may arise. The Pre-Event Planning Matrix is designed to help you choose the risks, hazards, or functions that are likely to be required by an event, and assign each to a primary agency (P) or a secondary or support agency (S). The functions and responsibility assignments must be discussed and decided in the planning stages, not when an incident occurs. This Pre-Event Planning Matrix is included on pages A-1 through A-3 of Appendix A: Job Aids. A Special Event Planning Checklist is included on pages A-4 through A-8 of Appendix A: Job Aids.

PROMOTER/SPONSOR(S)

The promoter or sponsor must be involved in all of the planning phases to ensure a successful event. Often, the promoter is interested in monetary gain more than he or she is interested in public safety. If this appears to be his or her primary goal, local agency participation is essential. You may encourage the promoter to cooperate by linking attendance at planning meetings with the permit process and issuance. For example, the permit to host the event may require the promoter's presence at the initial planning meeting. Teamwork promotes successful events.

One way to ensure public safety at an event is to follow the relevant laws or regulations of the community. Following these laws and regulations ensures that the promoter will keep the public's safety at the forefront of all plans. Some communities or States have public agency regulatory oversight of the promoter built into the permit process. For example, the community may have a requirement for the promoter to have adequate contingency plans in place before approving an event.

A Promoter/Sponsor Checklist is included on pages A-9 through A-21 of Appendix A: Job Aids.

RELEVANT LAWS OR REGULATIONS

Event promoters must usually gain approval from local, and sometimes even State, authorities to hold public events. The following information should be available to the promoters before beginning the permit-approval process:

- Identity of the approving authority and any other authorities actively involved in the approval process.
- Relevant statutes, ordinances, codes, and standards (i.e., life safety codes) existing for mass gatherings.
- Documentation required to support their application.
- Insurance, bond, liability issues.
- Relevant deadlines for the filing of applications.

Some communities offer a "One Stop Shopping" concept for permitting. The person requesting a permit for an event completes applications at one place and the information is forwarded to the appropriate agencies for their approval. The person requesting the permit does not have to track down the appropriate agencies to make a request. This concept also ensures that all required agencies are notified and considerations are made before the permit is issued.

Promoters should be aware of the approving authority's timetable for approving events and issuing permits and should include any potential delay in the event planning schedule.

As a condition for receiving approval, promoters may be required to provide feedback on the approval process and submit an evaluation before, during, and after the event, as needed. Promoters may be required to give feedback in the form of a debrief or a report to relevant authorities.

An Approving Authority Checklist is included on pages A-22 through A-32 of Appendix A: Job Aids.

LEGAL ISSUES

Some form of legislation usually governs or restricts public events or aspects of them. Some events, particularly extremely large or high-impact events, require special State or local legislation. Local ordinances provide health and medical guidelines.

Promoters should consider obtaining legal advice early in the planning stage. Items that warrant consideration include:

- Liability for injuries.
- Liability for acts or omissions.
- Liability for financial obligations incurred in responding to major emergencies occasioned by the event.
- Potential liability for the resultant effects of the event on normal emergency operations.

Permits may be required for parades, the sale and consumption of alcohol, pyrotechnics, and the sale of food items. Fire safety inspections should be required. Permission may also be required if it will be necessary to close certain adjacent or peripheral roads or streets. A permit may be required for the mass gathering itself.

Most public sector agencies have adopted a "User Pays" policy for services provided at sporting and entertainment events. The purpose of this policy is to improve the allocation of statute resources in the general community by providing a means of charging for services deployed to plan for, and respond to, sporting and entertainment events. Event promoters should consult local and State authorities to determine relevant fee structures and charges for services provided, including payment of overtime costs for personnel.

Promoters may be required to post a bond or provide liability insurance to cover the costs of response to emergencies, subsequent venue cleanup, traffic and crowd control, and other policing functions.

The head of the planning team must monitor the progress that is made in satisfying all legal requirements throughout the planning stage of the event.

In addition, research should be done in advance to determine statutory authority and emergency powers (i.e., isolation/quarantine, emergency evacuation, etc.) of the various parties involved.

POLITICAL ISSUES

Often communities have to deal with local political considerations when they plan events. No specific advice can be given to the promoter except to warn him or her that political considerations are always important to the local community. Often a way to encourage elected political officials to support an event is to show the monetary or quality-of-life impact that a successful event would have on their communities or careers. Explaining the positive impact encourages officials to support the public safety coordinators by providing adequate local resources and funding.

POLITICAL ISSUES (CONTINUED)

Any event has the potential to become an incident of national significance as that term is described in the National Response Plan (NRP). Recent revisions to Federal guidance documents indicate that any number of factors could escalate a local incident to an incident of national significance. Local planners must also be prepared to deal with a rapid transition of their incident to an incident of national significance.

ECONOMIC ISSUES

Special events often bring attention and significant economic benefits and opportunities to local communities. These could include an influx of revenue into the local community, such as the hotel and restaurant industry.

Local event planners must not sacrifice public safety for the sake of economic benefit. Certain businesses in a community may be adversely affected by certain requirements of the special event, such as closing streets in a commercial area or increased traffic in residential areas. Additional staffing may be required to ensure that service calls by local emergency services agencies are not hampered.

ATTENDEE/CROWD ISSUES

1. **Crowds are complex social structures.**

    Crowd roles:

    - Active Core: carry out action of crowd.
    - Cheerleaders: provide oral support for leaders.
    - Observers: follow actions but rarely take part.

    Significance of crowds:

    - Increase the probability of a dangerous occurrence.
    - Increase the potential number of victims.
    - Make communication slower and more difficult.
    - Make changes in action slower and more difficult.
    - Diffuse responsibility (someone else will do it).

2. **Panics and Crazes**

    Panic in a group is the flight from a real or perceived threat from which escape appears to be the only effective response. What appears to be panic is usually the result of poor inputs (especially communications or the lack of) and previous knowledge and experience.

    Craze in a group is the temporary, short-lived competitive rush by a group toward some attractive object. A craze tends to occur on entering an event, and may be exacerbated by the lack of information.

<u>**ATTENDEE/CROWD ISSUES (CONTINUED)**</u>

3. Deindividualization

Deindividualization is defined as a loss of self-awareness and evaluation apprehension in group situations that foster anonymity. Behavior may include:

- Mild lessening of restraint (e.g., screaming during a concert).
- Impulsive self-gratification (e.g., theft, vandalism, molestation).
- Destructive social explosions (e.g., group violence, rioting and torturing).

4. Defusing

The tedium that may be created by waiting and/or by the perception that other gates are being opened first, or later arrivals are being admitted first can create problems. Such things as appropriate music, the use of humor, food and beverage services moving through the group, cheerful security staff moving through the group, and good communication that includes a public address system, can help defuse the situation.

CROWD TYPES

CROWD TYPE[1]	COMMENT
AMBULATORY	Walking, usually calm
DISABILITY/LIMITED MOVEMENT	Crowd has limited or restricted movement; requires additional planning
COHESIVE/SPECTATOR	Watching specific activity
EXPRESSIVE/REVELOUS	Emotional release, for example, cheering movement in unison
PARTICIPATORY	Involved in actual event, for example, community fun runs
AGGRESSIVE/HOSTILE	Initially verbal, open to lawlessness
DEMONSTRATOR	Organized to some degree, for example, pickets, marches
ESCAPE/TRAMPLING	Danger may be real or imaginary
DENSE/SUFFOCATING	Reduction of individual physical movement
RUSHING/LOOTING	Attempt to acquire/obtain/steal something, for example, tickets
VIOLENT	Attacking/terrorizing

One crowd may exhibit all or part of the above types; therefore, you must consider each category, or at the least the most likely categories, in your plan.

[1] Table modified from Berlonghi, Alexander E. "Understanding and Planning for Different Spectator Crowds." *Engineering for Crowd Safety*. Ed. R.A. Smith and J.F. Dickie. Elsevier Science Publications B.V., 1993.

CROWD COMPOSITION

ASSESSMENT[2]	COMMENT
HOW ORGANIZED	For example, walking to venue versus demonstrators
LEADERSHIP	Normal crowd has no leadership; they are spontaneous.
COHESIVENESS	Degree of bonding
UNITY OF PURPOSE	Some may be focused; others have own agenda, for example, moshing or slam dancing.
COMMON MOTIVE FOR ACTION	Note distinction between performing same action (for example, cheering) versus motive for same action (for example, leaving the venue).
PSYCHOLOGICAL UNITY	Crowds at benefits are psychologically united for good; however, demonstrators could pose problems if antagonized.
EMOTIONAL INTENSITY	Much of this depends on the event and or special effects taking place.
VOLATILITY	To what degree has crowd reached an explosive point?
INDIVIDUAL BEHAVIOR	How much individual control and responsibility are being exercised? The more this is evident, the more restrained the crowd.
GROUP BEHAVIOR	To what degree are individuals dominated by the group? The more this is evident, the closer to "mob mentality."
DEGREE OF LAWLESSNESS	How much criminal behavior is taking place?
LEVEL OF VIOLENCE	Can be assessed historically and/or by current observations
LEVEL OF PROPERTY DAMAGE	How much is likely to occur and where, for example, parking area, toilets, walkways, etc.? Assessment is historical for venue, event, and crowd, plus current assessment.
LIKELIHOOD OF INJURY OR DEATH	Certain places at certain times, for example, major sporting event; and certain events, for example, motor races
NEED FOR CROWD CONTROL	How important is a detailed plan? Must be discussed with experts and experienced persons because the more detailed and complex the plan, the more expensive and resource-intense the commitment.

When you understand what you are dealing with, then brief ALL personnel on what to look for and how they should respond while they are performing their duties.

---

[2] Ibid.

CROWD CATALYSTS

CATALYST[3]	EXAMPLE
OPERATIONAL	Parking, no-show performers, cancellations
EVENT ACTIVITIES	Smoke, fire, lasers, noise
PERFORMER(S) ACTIONS	Sexual/violent gestures, challenges/song lyrics
SPECTATOR FACTORS	Drugs, alcohol, rush for seats
SECURITY FACTORS	Excessive or unreasonable force, abuse of authority
SOCIAL FACTORS	Racial tensions, team rivalries
WEATHER	Heat, humidity, rain, lack of ventilation
NATURAL DISASTER	Earthquake, deluge of rain, flash flood
MAN-MADE DISASTER	Structural failure, toxic substance

CRITICAL CROWD DENSITIES

The objective should be to prevent the build-up of large accumulations of patrons, particularly within short time periods, in confined spaces—especially if they are frustrated by the inability to see what is happening.

A study by Fruin (1981) identifies critical crowd densities as a common characteristic of crowd disasters. Critical crowd densities are approached when the floor space per standing person is reduced to about 5.38 square feet.

---

[3] Ibid.

CRITICAL CROWD DENSITIES (CONTINUED)

Considering the various movements or the positions that spectators will occupy, approximate minimal mobility requirements have been empirically identified by Fruin (1981) as follows:

- Pedestrians moving in a stream require average areas of 24.73 square feet per person to attain normal walking speed, and to pass and avoid others.
- At 10 square feet per person, walking becomes significantly restricted, and speeds noticeably reduced.
- At 4.95 square feet per person, the maximum capacity of a corridor or walkway is attained with movement at a shuffling gait and movement possible only as a group. This would be characteristic of a group exiting a stadium or theater.
- At less than 4.95 square feet per person average, individual pedestrian mobility becomes increasingly restricted.
- At approximately 3 square feet per person, involuntary contact and brushing against others occurs. This is a behavioral threshold generally avoided by the public, except in crowded elevators and buses.
- Below 2 square feet per person, potentially dangerous crowd forces and psychological pressures begin to develop.

Fruin (1981) contends that "the combined pressure of massed pedestrians and shock-wave effects that run through crowds at critical density levels produce forces which are impossible for individuals, even small groups of individuals, to resist."

The above information shows that you may need to provide a monitoring system, such as closed circuit television monitoring of crowd movements, that will provide warning to event personnel that they must take necessary action to prevent a major incident.

CROWD THROUGHPUT CAPACITIES

In his writings on crowd disasters, Fruin (1981) identifies several areas regarding spectator throughput in entry to a performance. For planning purposes, he suggests:

1. Ticket Collectors

Ticket collectors must be in a staff uniform or otherwise identifiable. Ticket collectors faced with a constant line can throughput a maximum of:

- One patron per second per portal in a simple pass-through situation.
- Two seconds per patron if the ticket must be torn and stub handed to the patron.

More complicated ticketing procedures (and/or answering the occasional question) will protract time per patron.

2. Doorways

A free-swinging door, open portal, or gate can accommodate up to one person per second with a constant queue.

Revolving doors and turnstiles would allow half this rate of throughput, or less.

CROWD THROUGHPUT CAPACITIES (CONTINUED)

3. Corridors, Walkways, Ramps
Have a maximum pedestrian traffic capacity of approximately 25 persons per minute per 1 foot of clear width, in dense crowds.

4. Stairs
Have a maximum practical traffic capacity of approximately 16 persons per minute in the upward direction. Narrow stairs (less than 5 feet) will lower the maximum flow.

5. Escalators and Moving Walkways
A standard 3.94-ft. wide escalator or moving walkway, operating at 118 feet per minute can carry 100 persons per minute under a constant queue.

EVENT CANCELLATION OR POSTPONEMENT

From time to time, an event may need to be canceled, postponed, or interrupted. If a crowd has already gathered, these actions have the potential to create dangerous crowd reactions. Have plans in place to manage an angry crowd appropriately and to address the possible readmission of patrons to the venue.

One major aspect to consider is authority to cancel or postpone an event. During the planning phase, the promoter and the planning team must discuss who has the authority to cancel or postpone an event as well as when and under what conditions the event can be postponed or canceled. These decisions must be made before the event begins, and everyone must know who has the authority. ICS is an excellent tool to ensure chain of command, communications, and proper approving authority.

Venue/Site

You may need to consider a number of alternative venues for an event. Emergency managers may be able to recommend appropriate venues based on health and safety considerations.

Finding a suitable venue or set of venues can be difficult. Answering the following questions during the planning stage can aid in the selection of an appropriate event site:

- Will staging the event require multiple venues?
- Is this kind of event normally conducted at a fixed facility?
- Will a fixed facility be used in ways that may not be considered normal for that facility?
- Is the event regularly conducted at a temporary venue?
- Is the event a "one-of-a-kind" project at a temporary venue?
- What services and utilities are available at the venue?
- What additional services and utilities will be required at the venue?
- Is there a need for backup services or utilities (i.e., redundant systems)?

A universal map/grid referencing system for the entire event footprint should be developed in advance for all attendees and event staff (including public safety personnel) to allow for the rapid identification of event-specific facilities and other locations in an emergency.

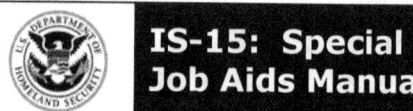
Venue/Site (Continued)

- What shelter facilities are available at the following locations:

  - Transport pick-up and drop-off areas?
  - Spectator and official viewing areas?
  - Seated eating areas?
  - Pedestrian thoroughfares?
  - First aid and medical centers?
  - Competitors' and officials' marshaling areas?

- What is the duration of the event, and will it continue during the hours of darkness?
- Have you provided for the needs of people with disabilities?
- Does the date of the event conflict with other events to be conducted in the area?
- Will seasonal weather require any special contingency planning?
- Have you surveyed the proposed site (particularly outdoor sites) for inherent hazards associated with the location, and have any been identified? Do utility lines that could be brought down by a severe storm traverse the site? Is the site adjacent to a waterway prone to flooding?
- Is the site layout such that, in the event of a mass casualty incident, space is available for an onsite triage area to permit stabilizing medical treatment before critical patients are transported to local health care facilities? Is such an area accessible to ambulances to eliminate the need for carrying patients long distances?
- Does the site allow for mass decontamination considerations?
- Have site emergency evacuation considerations been addressed?
- Does the site allow for adequate crowd regulation by means of, for example, existing regimented seating areas or flow barriers?
- Are spectator overflow areas available to prevent crowd crush if spectator turnout significantly exceeds expectations, a common phenomenon at rock concerts?
- In an urban setting, as is characteristic of a stadium venue, could the adjacent streets on all sides be closed to other than emergency service, and resident vehicles, creating a perimeter for access as well as a buffer zone?
- Is a staging area for protestors necessary? Is it required?

Criminal and Terrorist Risks

Special events and mass gatherings are a perfect target because of the large number of people, media coverage, and the high-profile impact if a terrorist strikes. Small communities and their events may actually be attractive sites for terrorists because the residents may believe they are not at risk and so do not prepare themselves. However, event planners can take steps to prepare for the same risks that all communities face.

Prepare public safety personnel to protect themselves. Ensure that your community's public safety personnel are adequately trained and equipped with personal protective equipment (PPE) as dictated by their response role to protect themselves as they help others.

Criminal and Terrorist Risks (Continued)

Some events may appeal to terrorists for a number of reasons, including an anniversary date, religious holiday, a particular location, the nature of the event, or those who will be included among the participants. Communities can identify terrorist organizations that may be attracted to their event for any number of reasons and can prepare accordingly. Knowledge is an advantage. Know the possible risks that the event poses and the audience that the event will attract. Ensure that your public safety teams are prepared and have practiced their response to both terrorism and suspected terrorism, and that they understand how to mitigate any potential terrorist incidents.

Every jurisdiction in the country has conducted a jurisdiction threat and vulnerability assessment, which was required by the Federal Government as part of the national homeland security preparedness effort. When event planners formulate contingency plans for special events, they should work together with State and Federal partners and ensure that State and local data from these Federally mandated assessments are reviewed. Local law enforcement professionals should consult the FBI and State law enforcement intelligence specialists on current threat and vulnerability data as part of the event planning process. The current Homeland Security Advisory System threat level should be considered, and event planners should prepare for contingencies if the Federal threat level changes during the event.

THREAT ASSESSMENT

Planning and intelligence gathering are necessary activities for law enforcement personnel during event planning. The level of commitment to these anti-terrorist activities influences the level of response capabilities that should be maintained.

Two terms that event planners should understand are anti-terrorism and counter-terrorism:

- Anti-terrorism is a term used to define actions taken to mitigate potential effects of terrorist activity.
- Counter-terrorism is best defined as operational actions taken or activities planned to prevent a terrorist activity or event.

TARGETS

Most targets singled out by terrorist groups fall into one of eleven critical infrastructure areas or five key asset areas:

Critical Infrastructure

- Agriculture/food supplies
- Water
- Public health systems
- Emergency services (police, fire, EMS)
- Military targets/defense industry
- Cyber-terrorism and information
- Energy infrastructure
- Transportation infrastructure
- Banking/Finance
- Chemical and hazardous materials
- Postal/shipping facilities

Key Assets

- Monuments or public icons
- Nuclear power plants
- Dams
- Government facilities
- Other commercial key assets

MOTIVES

The motives of extremist groups can generally be identified as:

- Political
- Religious
- Racial
- Environmental
- Special interest

WEAKNESSES IN MEASURING THREAT

Terrorist threats are often difficult to measure because they are:

- Dynamic
- Mobile
- Difficult to recognize (lone offenders, splinter groups)
- Dependent upon the ease and availability of creating a WMD device
- Difficult to quantify, or subjective (open to interpretation, with a tendency toward inflating results)

WEAKNESSES IN MEASURING THREAT (CONTINUED)

The dangers of information sharing (outside of those who have a "need to know") also make it difficult to measure the extent of the threat because unauthorized disclosure of information may:

- Lead to the violation of operational security.
- Create unnecessary panic.
- Produce unintended media attention.

CONTEMPORARY TERRORISM

In the past, we wanted to believe that terrorism was something that happened outside of the United States. Unfortunately, this is no longer the case. The FBI has determined that contemporary terrorists have generally:

- Been politically motivated.
- Sought and used publicity to gain recognition and public sentiment.
- Most often viewed, trained, and equipped themselves as an army at war.
- Sought to cross jurisdictional lines to further confound law enforcement detection and apprehension.
- Had the support and funding of national governments from outside of the United States.
- Invited public scrutiny to put law enforcement on trial by the effective use of the media.

CHAPTER 2: EVENT OPERATIONAL CONSIDERATIONS

INTRODUCTION

While planning an event, it is important to consider every possible risk and hazard that may occur. This chapter covers most of the basic risks that may be encountered at an event. The responsibilities for dealing with these risks vary with each jurisdiction, and every community needs to have a plan listing who or what organization will respond to the anticipated risks or hazards. Knowing the risks ahead of time and planning for those risks are essential to successful planning. Planning for the worst may help reduce the chance of a "worst-case scenario" happening. If the responding agency knows the risks ahead of time and is alert, it can reduce its response time, ensuring the safety and security of those in attendance. Risks vary depending upon the type of event; therefore, event organizers must tailor the planning for each risk to the specific event.

The promoter is one source of information on potential risks that may be faced at the event. The promoter should be aware of the support services that are needed to respond to any incident and the availability of those services in the community. If event organizers know the possible risks that an event poses and the nature of the audience that is likely to attend the event, they can analyze the hazards and take the necessary steps to plan a safe event.

HAZARD ANALYSIS

Hazard analysis provides planners with information about the kinds of emergencies that may occur and their potential consequences. Analysis assists planners in deciding what steps to take to prevent the possible emergencies and how to respond if an incident occurs.

The best way to begin a hazard analysis is to list the possible risks present at the event. Every community's list will differ based on topographical and geographical features, weather patterns, and other factors. (Tsunami, for example, would not be identified as a hazard in an area that is far from a coastline.) Identifying hazards also includes considering the possibility of a secondary hazard (for example, a tornado may lead to power failure, loss of water, and other hazards).

The following table includes some of the more obvious risks and possible hazards that may exist. Being prepared for the worst allows planners to have responders and supplies on hand if an emergency does occur.

HAZARD ANALYSIS (CONTINUED)

Typical List of Risks and Hazards	
Abandoned vehicles	Hurricane
Airplane crash	Intentional chemical release
Airspace encroachment	Kidnapping
Assault	Landslide
Avalanche	Loss of utilities (water, sewer, telephone)
Biological incidents	Lost child
Bomb threat/suspicious package	Lost and found
Building inspection	Media relations
Cancellation of event	Motorcades
Civil disturbance with demonstrations	Mudslides
Communications	Parking
Credentials	Permitting
Crowd control	Power failure (sustained)
Cyber attacks	Radiological release
Dam failure	Security
Demonstrations	Structural collapse
Dignitary protection	Subsidence
Drought	Terrorism
Earthquake	Ticketing
Epidemic or other public health concern	Tornado
Evacuation of area	Traffic control
Explosive materials	Train derailment
Fire	Tsunami
First aid matters	Urban conflagration
Flood	Volcanic eruption
Food handling violations	Wildfire
Food waste disposal problems	Winter storm
Hazardous Materials release	
Hostage without terrorism	
Human waste disposal problems	

HAZARD ANALYSIS (CONTINUED)

Event planners must identify characteristics of each possible hazard to determine the risk and consequences. Characteristics to identify are:

- Frequency of occurrence—the frequency of occurrence (both historical and predicted) for each hazard in the particular jurisdiction.
- Magnitude and intensity—the projected severity of the hazard's occurrence.
- Location—the location of the hazard, if the hazard is associated with a facility or landscape feature.
- Spatial extent—the geographic area that may be expected to suffer the impact of the hazard (either around the known location of a hazard or as an estimate for non-localized hazards such as tornadoes).
- Duration—the length of time that the hazard may be expected to last.
- Seasonal pattern—times of the year when the hazard threat exists (based on month-by-month historical occurrence).
- Speed of onset and availability of warning—the amount of time projected between first warning (if any) and actual occurrence.

POTENTIAL CONSEQUENCES

To determine the potential consequences of a hazard, estimate the lives, property, and services at risk. Evaluate the extent of the hazard by closely examining your community in terms of:

- People (deaths, injuries, and displacement).
- Critical facilities (days of service loss, repair time).
- Community functions (disruption).
- Property (damage, destruction, cost of replacement or repair).
- Potential secondary hazards (dams, chemical processing plants).
- Loss of revenue.
- Negative public image of jurisdiction.

When evaluating hazards, remember that hazards may occur in multiples and that one hazard may cause a secondary hazard.

1. Identify the Hazards
   Determine what kinds of emergencies have occurred or could occur in the jurisdiction.

2. Weigh and Compare the Risks
   Determine the relative threat posed by the identified hazards, using qualitative and quantitative ratings. This information enables planners to decide which hazards merit special attention in planning and other emergency management efforts.

3. Profile Hazards and Their Potential Consequences
   Compile historical and predictive information on each of the hazards and overlay this information on community data to estimate the hazard's potential impact on the community.

POTENTIAL CONSEQUENCES (CONTINUED)

4. <u>Create and Apply Scenarios</u>
    For the top-ranked hazards (or those that rate above a certain threshold), develop scenarios that raise the hazard's development to the level of an emergency. This is a brainstorming activity that tracks the hazard from initial warning (if any) to its impact on a specific part of the jurisdiction and its generation of specific consequences. Brainstorming provides information about what actions and resources might be required for response.

The Job Aid, Hazard Vulnerability Assessment on pages A-55 through A-58 of Appendix A: Job Aids, provides a worksheet for the planning team to use as a starting point to identify specific hazards and risks for the event. This is a vital process to bring stakeholders together to brainstorm potential hazards and begin developing comprehensive planning strategies. There are other, more comprehensive, planning tools that are available to address specific needs that the planning team may identify from the Job Aid worksheet. Consult your local/State emergency management agencies for other planning tools.

CONTINGENCY PLANS

Unfortunately, not every event runs smoothly. Often, incidents occur that are beyond the control of the planning team. Therefore, contingency plans for every event should be in place.

An emergency response plan requires a comprehensive hazard and vulnerability analysis. Consultation among all parties who may respond to an emergency situation during the event is essential.

Some important questions related to ICS planning include:

- What weather conditions may require cancellation of the event?
- What weather conditions will postpone the event?
- How will storm warnings be monitored?
- What plans are in place for sudden, severe weather conditions, such as tornadoes? Will shelters be available?
- Who has the authority to make these decisions, and at what point does he or she exercise that authority?
- How is notification made of a cancellation or postponement?
- Are additional security personnel, including police, on standby or on call if an immediate increase in these services is required?
- Have you advised ambulance services and local hospitals of the nature of the event, provided an expected spectator profile, and estimated potential medical problems?
- Have you notified fire and rescue services of the nature of the event and identified the services that might be required?
- Has the jurisdiction considered how to respond to a Chemical, Biological, Radiological, Nuclear, Explosive (CBRNE) type of man-made, intentional event?
- Has the need for mass decontamination been considered?

CONTINGENCY PLANS (CONTINUED)

- Have any "target hardening" considerations been explored to increase the deterrence factor against man-made intentionally caused events?
- Have you identified the types of heavy equipment that could be required in a catastrophe (for example, a grandstand collapse)? Have you made plans to obtain that equipment at any time, including off-business hours?
- Have you advised counseling services of the nature of the event and identified the services that might be required?
- If the event is particularly dangerous, and deaths are a real possibility (for example, at automobile or power boat races or air shows), have you formulated plans to support any required coroner's investigation?
- To permit responders to precisely identify the location of an emergency quickly, address the following questions:

    - Will a grid-type venue plan be available, which is common to all emergency services, including access roads, pathways, major landmarks, spectator, performer and vendor areas?
    - Will vendor locations or booths be numbered and be included on the venue plan?

STRUCTURAL MATTERS

An area of great concern is the physical setup of the event. Planners need to consider what performance facilities are needed, what special structures are needed for indoor or outdoor events, and whether temporary structures can be used. These are just a few primary concerns.

STAGES, PLATFORMS, AND OTHER PERFORMANCE FACILITIES

When setting up an event, stages, platforms, and the other performance facilities are an area of major safety consideration. The type of event and its site affect the choice of performance equipment and its stability requirements. Qualified inspectors should perform some type of inspection to ensure that the structure is appropriate for the event and that the structure is safe.

The expected behavior of the crowd is one of the principal factors determining stage configuration. While classical music and ballet performances usually attract a mature and orderly audience, teenage and pre-teen fans at rock concerts have been known to storm the stage to touch their idols. Such incidents, apart from being disruptive, have caused injuries. Therefore, event planners should understand the emotional and physical character of the audience that a particular performance will attract.

STAGES, PLATFORMS, AND OTHER PERFORMANCE FACILITIES (CONTINUED)

There are three principal ways to gather information about the anticipated crowd:

- Review press reports and contact local public safety officials who were present at previous performances.
- Speak with spectators who have attended adolescent entertainment events such as rock concerts. In the past, spectators have provided valuable insights into what behavior authorities might expect from audiences for different entertainers.
- Check with the promoter to determine audience behavior at past events and the type of crowd and the behavior that can be expected.

Stages are usually elevated to provide the audience a better view of the performance, especially for spectators who are farther back. This elevation is itself a barrier to those who would rush the stage in an attempt to touch a performer. In addition, this increased height can create an area free of spectators at the base of the stage because the audience members will position themselves back from the stage so that their line of sight is not impeded.

At some venues first aid personnel are located under the stage to accept injuries occasioned at the front of the spectator area. A stage or a platform alone is usually insufficient to deter determined and agile spectators, however, and an additional physical barrier is needed in front of the stage.

INDOOR EVENTS

During concerts held indoors, an effective practice is to erect a "V" shaped barrier in front of the stage to deflect patrons away from the stage area if any surge comes from behind. The "V" shape also provides an additional barrier to prevent spectators from reaching the stage. Security staff can position themselves in this spectator-free zone or should be able to gain access to it quickly from either end of the stage.

Barrier posts must be securely anchored to the floor, not merely mounted to freestanding bases. They should also have some padded protection. Such a fence construction is usually engineered to provide a certain amount of "give" upon impact, thus reducing the potential for crush injuries as occasioned in the 2000 Denmark, Pearl Jam concert tragedy.

OUTDOOR EVENTS

Board fences similar to the "V" shaped barrier described for indoor concerts can be used in an outdoor setting. Board fences have the added benefit of providing a walk space on the spectator side of the fence as well as behind it. Because most outdoor concerts do not provide seating, spectators in the front rows seated on the ground have to take a position several yards back from the fence to permit them to see the stage over the top of the fence. This area permits emergency access to the front rows of spectators.

Any stage protection barrier must be designed to sustain a certain amount of flex in order to prevent the crushing of spectators in the front by a crowd surge from behind. At the same time, it must be sufficiently solid so that it will not collapse and cause injuries. Fences installed as stage barriers often fail to meet this two-fold requirement.

BREAK-AWAY STAGE SKIRTS

The front skirt around the base of a stage can be constructed to break away under the pressure of a crowd surge, thus allowing spectators to be pushed under the stage rather than be crushed against its base. This idea is not practical where there is less than six feet clearance beneath the stage, however, because of the potential for head injuries if a spectator collides with the leading edge of the stage.

It should be stressed that use of a breakaway stage skirt does not remove the requirement for a barrier in front of the stage and should be considered only as additional security if barriers fail.

EMERGENCY EVACUATION

There are physical structures designed for use in areas of egress that, in the event of an emergency where evacuation is required, collapse to allow for the maximum passthrough.

TEMPORARY STRUCTURES

Because of their transitory nature, many events require easily constructed temporary structures. These include the stage platform itself, as well as towers to house speakers and floodlights, temporary seating such as bleachers, dance platforms, roofs, towers and masts, viewing platforms, marquees and large tents, and decorative items such as archways, overhead signs, and even sideshows.

All such temporary structures must be designed and erected to include a margin for safety and a view to potential hazards. A local government building-codes inspector should supervise the erection of temporary structures and ensure that they conform to local government building or engineering specifications.

Temporary structures are often hurriedly erected because access to the venue may be permitted only a short time before the event opens and they are usually designed for rapid removal at the conclusion of the event. In addition, these temporary structures are frequently neither designed nor erected to withstand stresses other than from intended use and are therefore not engineered to incorporate safety features. High winds or spectators climbing for a better vantage point can overstress these structures.

Personnel should inspect temporary structures periodically during events of long duration. They should post warnings on, or close, a temporary structure whose intended purpose is being violated.

LOAD CAPACITY

All structures have load capacities, and precautions should be in place to prevent misuse through overloading. These precautions apply to any viewing platform or vantage point, such as building walkways or balconies, which can cause a major incident if the number of spectators upon these structures is not properly controlled.

The bases of temporary structures must be protected from damage by vehicular traffic through the use of designated buffer zones.

SEATING

Ideally, all seating should be reserved; however, this ideal situation may be difficult to achieve at outdoor events.

If most of the spectators are in their teenage years, provide seating to control surges and crushing at the front of the stage. A security presence to ensure that audience members do not stand on seats is also recommended. Seating should be adequately anchored to prevent its movement.

Another area of concern is the spacing of the seats, and local life-safety codes may define acceptable practices in this area. The seating should be spaced far enough apart to allow emergency crews access to patients. Often, grouping the seats and providing large walkways between the groups is a way to provide this access.

TEMPORARY SEATING AND ANCHORAGE

Seating in a community center, arena, or similar indoor location often combines fixed perimeter seating with additional foldable or stackable seating on the central floor.

Temporary seats are often not secured to the floor or to one another. While this may not present any problems with certain audiences, more enthusiastic spectators may pose the following problems:

- Persons standing on the seats for a better view are prone to injury because they may lose their balance or become jostled. In such instances, they can adversely affect other spectators, sometimes causing a "domino effect" in closely spaced chairs. The potential for a significant number of injuries exists.
- If an audience becomes hostile, portable chairs can be used as dangerous missiles. It is not uncommon for hostile fans to become aggressive and throw items. Seats that are not anchored become dangerous projectiles.

Portable, folding, or stacking chairs should be secured to the floor. Where this is not possible, attach the legs of each row of chairs to two long planks, one running under the front pairs of legs and one running under the back, as an alternative solution.

A Building Department Venue Assessment Checklist is included on pages A-44 through A-46 of Appendix A: Job Aids.

HIGH-PROFILE/CONTROVERSIAL EVENTS

Because of the nature of the event, the crowd composition, or for other reasons, certain events cause more controversy and create greater risks than others do. For example, events involving groups that hold controversial beliefs present a greater risk for criminal or terrorist behavior. Events involving high-level officials are also at a greater risk for terrorist activity because of the significance of the official and the high-profile visibility of the participants and those in attendance. On some occasions, if the date of the event coincides with the anniversary of another terrorist event, the date of the event itself may be considered controversial. Planners must consider every reason why an event may promote controversy or attract special attention.

Conflicts will exist between public safety, recovery, and criminal investigation agencies during terrorist incidents. Rescue and recovery issues and actions must be separated from criminal investigation issues and actions before the event occurs, and non-law enforcement workers should be given training on matters of evidence. Evidence teams should be created to practice and train with local emergency responders and epidemiologic investigators to promote mutual understanding of one another's roles.

PROTESTORS

If organizers anticipate that a mass gathering or special event will attract the attention of organized protest groups, they should meet, if possible, with the leaders of those groups in advance. The organizers and group leaders can discuss ground rules of acceptable behaviors and the anticipated public safety response to criminal or disruptive behavior by local law enforcement agencies. Building rapport by gaining a mutual understanding of what to expect can decrease the likelihood of disruptive behavior, or at least ensure that everyone knows what will and will not be tolerated. Many jurisdictions have a permitting process that is required for this type of activity.

Protestors who arrive spontaneously should also be planned for, and in many cases may become a law enforcement issue if the permit process has been violated. Many times, these groups hold extremist views or specific concerns about a particular issue that may be tied to the event.

SPECTATOR MANAGEMENT AND CROWD CONTROL

This chapter has discussed the hazards associated with structural design and integrity, but what about the dangers that may be created by the participants themselves? The aim of spectator management and crowd control is to maintain order, prevent deviation from desired behavior, and re-establish order if it breaks down, thereby ensuring maximum enjoyment for the assembled gathering. Event organizers are responsible for spectator management and crowd control; however, this function passes to local authorities, such as police, fire, and emergency medical services, when the situation is beyond the resources and capability of the organizers. Knowing what to expect from a given audience can lessen risks and hazards from the crowd itself. Event organizers should research lessons learned from previous events and have appropriate response plans in place before the event takes place.

Spectator management refers to planning and preparation issues, such as ticket sales and collection, admittance and inspection, ushering, seating, parking, public announcements, toilets, and washrooms.

Crowd control refers to mechanisms that are used to reinstate order, such as limited access control, admission control, and arrests.

A crowd is defined as any number of people coming together in any place for any reason. Crowds gather daily in shopping centers, airports, and stadiums, and occasionally in places that are not designed specifically for large numbers of people.

In the planning process for a forthcoming event, organizers must have an understanding of both individual and crowd dynamics and how these elements interrelate. While this is a preliminary guide to crowd control problems that organizers most frequently encounter, planners need to expand upon the particular issues for each crowd and venue. You may find additional information on crowd control in other literature and press reports; from the promoter; private security organizations; police, fire, and emergency medical authorities; and, for visiting dignitaries, from personal security services and government agencies. All of this information will assist in predicting potential problems that you can then address in the planning process.

GENERAL ISSUES FOR CONSIDERATION

Major crowd issues you should address include:

- Size—Maximum numbers permitted are often established by regulation for safety reasons.
- Demographics—Consider the composition of the audience, including the age and gender mix. If you identify in advance that young children will constitute a high proportion of the audience, consider additional facilities, such as childcare, family bathrooms, and rental strollers. Audiences made up of young children or elderly people tend to require additional medical facilities, and children and the elderly are more susceptible to crush injury than teens or adults.

Different kinds of events may attract certain types of spectators that require special attention. Consider the following:

- Rock concerts, in contrast to other types of concerts, may experience a higher incidence of problems with drug and alcohol abuse, underage drinking, and possession of weapons.
- Religious and "faith healing" events may attract a significant number of ill and infirm people, which may increase the need for onsite medical care.
- Events for senior citizens may also require higher levels of health services.
- Certain sports events may attract over-reactive and violent supporters.
- Cultural events may require special arrangements, including the provision of interpreter services, special food services, and multilingual signposting, brochures, and announcements.

- Outdoor Concerts—additional considerations:

  - Control and distribution of spectators in the field.
  - Suggested minimum space allocation of 4 to 5 square feet per person on grounds with no seats.
  - Some form of sectoring and barrier management by security is important.

ENTRANCES AND EXITS

Important considerations for the entry and exit of spectators include:

Entrances

The primary function of entrances is to provide:

- For supervision, marshaling and directing crowds.
- Access for emergency services.
- Egress and evacuation routes.
- Initial surveillance and inspection of attendees (i.e., magnetometers).

ENTRANCES AND EXITS (CONTINUED)

Entrances should also:

- Be clearly signposted.
- Be in working order.
- Be compliant with the Americans With Disabilities Act (ADA); and
- Provide for separation of pedestrian and vehicular traffic.

Entrance Management—Event organizers should:

- Permit flexible opening and closing times. (Advertised times are recommended, however.)
- Stagger entry times by providing supporting activities.
- Keep entrances clear of all other activities.
- Keep lines away from entrances.
- Ensure there are sufficient numbers of suitable barriers, fences, gates, and turnstiles.
- Locate ticket sales and pick-up points in line with, but separate from entrances.
- Arrange to have a public address system or alternative communications system to provide information and entertainment to the crowd waiting at the entrance.
- Consider the potential need for medical and security personnel presence.
- Provide sufficient numbers of personnel who are appropriately trained.
- Ensure that control points for searches to detect prohibited items, such as alcohol, social drugs, glass, metal containers, and weapons, are in place and do not affect movement.
- Provide a secure area for the storage of confiscated goods.
- Provide toilets, if lines are expected to be long.
- Apply metering techniques as appropriate.

Exit Management—Event organizers should:

- Ensure that exit doors are not locked. If personnel are concerned about illegal entry, then doors could be fitted with alarms.
- Ensure that exit doors open in the direction of escape and are confirmed as operational.
- Check the placement, function, and signposting of exits.
- Ensure that doors that do not lead to an exit are so marked, preventing "dead end" entrapment and the potential for panic.
- Ensure that all exit corridors are free of all impediments to crowd movement.
- Ensure that turnstiles are freewheeling or can operate in reverse.
- Ensure that cords, which can create trip hazards, do not cross exit corridors. (If this precaution is unavoidable, the cord should be marked, insulated, and secured to the floor to prevent damage and potential electrical risks.)

Escalator Management—Event organizers should provide for:

- Staff control at the top and bottom, including an emergency stop button.
- Metering of the flow at both ends.

ENTRANCES AND EXITS (CONTINUED)

Stairway/Corridor Management—Event organizers should provide for:

- Control of both ends if the crowd is large.
- Metering that may be required for safety.

CREDENTIALING

The mission of special events credentialing is to design and produce badge identification to ensure the greatest possible level of security for personnel and property, and to enhance the ability of law enforcement personnel to control access to secure areas, facilities, and events.

A credential identifies specific individuals who require access to a venue(s) to perform an operational role or function, whereas a ticket is issued to spectators or other members of the general public who do not perform an operational role or function.

In essence, a credential is equivalent to an "Incident Badge." A "ticket" is NOT a "credential."

Credentialing provides sufficient information to verify the identity of the bearer and his or her level of access, and should include security features to prevent counterfeiting and assist in credential verification.

Event planners tasked with credentialing may wish to consider the following:

- Who will be credentialed?
- Will credentialed personnel require police record checks?
- Who will conduct the record checks?
- What criteria will be used for various levels of access?
- Who will have the final decision on who will or will not be credentialed?
- Who will be responsible for credential production?
- Who will authorize credential production?
- What is the format for the receipt of the information necessary to produce the credential (e.g., electronic, paper)?
- Will a photograph be needed?
- Where will the credentialing center be located? (The credentialing center should be located outside of the secure zone and accessible to those requiring credentials.)
- Who will secure this location and provide security for personnel and equipment?
- How will the security of the credentialing database be maintained?
- How, and to whom, will credentials be distributed?

TICKETING

Ticketing is the first means of achieving crowd control. Essential matters to address include the following:

- If advance ticketing is possible, it is preferred because it allows organizers to anticipate audience numbers and plan accordingly. It also enables them to pass on information about needed services (for example, parking, traffic patterns, first aid, water sources, toilets, and personal needs) to ticket-holders before the event.
- When multiple entrances to the venue are provided, directing spectators to arrive via specific entrances can reduce congestion.
- If it is feasible, stagger crowd arrival by specifying entry times. Again, this plan reduces congestion at entrances.

BARRIERS

Effective use of barriers can prevent many problems, including congestion in thoroughfares and walkways. Questions that you should consider in the planning phase include the following:

- What types of barriers are required? Is a solid physical barrier required, or would a psychological barrier, such as barrier tape, suffice? The use of psychological barriers is suitable only for orderly crowds. Any physical barrier must be able to withstand crowd surges.
- How will personnel respond if the barrier is breached?
- Can barriers be used to section the crowd and create passages for emergency personnel to evacuate ill or injured spectators?
- Will barriers be used to create a "pit" between the crowd and the stage, which can be used to facilitate the evacuation of injured spectators?
- Can barriers be easily dismantled by the crowd and used for other purposes?

There are physical structures designed for use in areas of egress that, in the event of an emergency where evacuation is required, collapse to allow for the maximum passthrough.

A Public Works Department Checklist is included on pages A-42 and A-43 of Appendix A: Job Aids.

DEFUSING CROWD TENSION

The tedium that is created by an extended wait in line for tickets or admission can be a precursor for crowd control problems. Such boredom can create or magnify tempers, particularly if, with little distraction, those in line perceive other doors being opened first or other patrons getting in at the head of the line.

The following means of defusing anger have been used with success in different venues:

- Up-tempo music (of a type consistent with the age group of the crowd) played over the public address system.
- Humorous, animal-costumed individual, such as a mascot, walking up and down the line giving handshakes, pats, and waves.
- Large inflated beach ball, which is lobbed back and forth over, and by, the spectators;
- Food and beverage sellers moving through the group.
- Cheerful security staff, passing up and down the line, talking to people.

Introducing some of these same distractions inside the event can calm a potentially agitated crowd.

In addition, a mascot conducting a spectator sing-along to up-tempo music or a ticket or program number draw on the field for the last ball used at a sporting event can alleviate tension in a crowd.

Whenever possible, spectators should be informed before an event of any special conditions or arrangements for the event, such as parking, clothing, food and drink, sunscreen, shelter, and alcohol restrictions. Notice of special conditions or arrangements may be distributed via advertisements or in leaflets accompanying tickets.

Outdoor events, sometimes spread over large areas, require further considerations, such as:

- Toilet facilities located outside gates and between disembarkation points and the venue.
- Shelter.
- Telephone facilities.

The venue should allow adequate regulation of crowd movement, such as adequate exiting from ticketed seating areas and sectoring and flow barriers, including barriers to separate vehicles from pedestrians.

Spectator overflow areas should be available to prevent crushing. Contingency plans are required in case spectator turnout significantly exceeds expectations. This phenomenon is common at rock concerts. This may be more of an issue for outside venues, as life safety codes for inside venues may help address maximum crowd attendance.

RESTRICTED VIEWING LOCATIONS

Clear lines of vision for spectators are important to reduce the likelihood that crowds will move to get a better view of the stage. Also, a wide angle of view helps to reduce crowd densities in front of the stage. If restricted viewing is unavoidable, tickets for spectators in those sections should note this fact.

VIDEO SCREENS

Video or projection screens aid in crowd management because they can provide:

- Entertainment before and between acts.
- Information concerning facilities and important messages including public safety and traffic messages for both inside and outside the venue.
- Close-up vision of on-stage action for spectators as a means of reducing crowd movement toward the stage.

TRAFFIC AND TRANSPORTATION

Transportation presents one of the first impressions that attendees will have about an event's organization, command, and control. Sitting in a line of cars for hours on the highway to gain access to an event will undoubtedly create a negative impression. The traffic from the event may not merely affect the local traffic but the traffic in the entire region. Planners should ensure that the surrounding communities are aware of the event and the potential impact on traffic in their area.

Depending on the scope and size of the event, traffic may be a routine issue. For example, many sports stadiums hire professional traffic planners to provide guidance on the most efficient ways to facilitate access and egress to various parking lots, and have procedures in place that adequately handle traffic flow on a regular basis.

The promoter is responsible for any traffic disruption that is associated with the event and should be held accountable by the permitting authority. The permitting authority can require the promoter to work with local public safety and traffic service providers to create contingency plans to minimize negative traffic impacts on the community at large.

At a minimum, local law enforcement, departments of transportation and public works, the local media, any existing public transportation authorities, and the promoter should comprise a traffic management group who must begin traffic planning well in advance of the event. The group should use the local media to inform residents in advance of the expected impact that the event will have on their mobility.

Being straightforward with the local community about anticipated problems or congestion areas will minimize the negative impact on local traffic service agencies. Many residents, when advised in advance to do so, will avoid certain areas or take alternate routes so that their movement is not impeded or prolonged.

TRAFFIC AND TRANSPORTATION (CONTINUED)

Traffic and transportation concerns that traffic management must address include:

- Does the site have adequate access and staging areas for large numbers of emergency vehicles in the event of a major incident?
- What impact will weather conditions have on transportation?
- What type of road leads to the event? Paved? Gravel? Dirt?
- Is access to, and the road network within, the site adequate to prevent emergency responders from having to walk significant distances to the principal spectator areas(s)?
- Is there sufficient room on the site (that is, for staging, manoeuvring) to permit repositioning or redeployment of emergency vehicles as dictated by the incident?
- Because of the nature of road access, would early arriving vehicles, such as ambulances, be prevented from leaving by gridlock produced by subsequently arriving equipment?
- Is the site served by an access road or street that could be closed to the public and used only for expeditious emergency and service vehicle ingress and egress?
- If access roads are unpaved, would emergency vehicles become bogged down if heavy rains occurred during, or just prior to, the event?
- Is the surrounding road network able to handle the anticipated spectator vehicular traffic?
- If spectator-parking areas are filled, will the road network allow continued vehicle flow, thus preventing gridlock?
- Is signposting, including gate numbering, clearly established inside and outside the venue?
- Are communications systems inside and outside the venue capable of providing public announcements, marshaling instructions, and evacuation orders?
- Is a system in place to monitor crowd flow (as through the use of spotters or aviation resources)?
- Does the organization have additional towing vehicles available?

Where there may be health and safety implications, efficient management of crowd movement includes:

- Awareness of public transport congestion at road, rail, and water interchanges and, in some cases, at airports.
- Use of coaches and buses to reduce private vehicle traffic and any potential problems that large vehicles may present (for example access difficulties, parking requirements, potential road blockages).
- Alterations to normal traffic and road use.
- Traffic control.
- Adequacy of the surrounding road network to handle the anticipated spectator vehicular traffic before, during, and after the event.
- Communication between traffic management groups and other services, including the local media.
- Access and egress routes including:

  - Arrangements for people with disabilities.
  - Pedestrian access, including considerations of distance, terrain, surface, and lighting.
  - Designated pick-up and set-down points.

VEHICLE ACCESS AND EGRESS ROUTES

Consider the environmental hazards that may result if access and egress routes are not established for:

- Portable toilet pump-out.
- Garbage removal.
- Water tankers.
- Car parking.
- Ambulances.
- Law enforcement vehicles.
- Fire vehicles.
- EMS vehicles.
- Public works and utility vehicles.
- Other essential service vehicles.

SIGNAGE AND USE OF THE MEDIA

If organizers anticipate that event traffic will have a major impact on community surface streets, they should consider requiring the promoter to hire a professional traffic planner to work in conjunction with law enforcement and public works personnel to create alternate routing or special signage to and from the event. Strategically placed, variable-message signs on the highway that allow text messages to be changed by remote control are very useful devices to inform the motoring public. Temporary fixed signage can also be considered. The additional signs must adhere to the current industry standard and be easily understood by the public.

Additionally, using a local AM radio station or a specially designated frequency to broadcast travel information and instructions from the Public Safety Incident Command Post to arriving or departing patrons on the day of the event can help to lower their frustration. Broadcasting is also a means for event command and control staff to provide patrons with useful guidance and safety messages prior to their arrival. Much useful information, such as traffic routing and identification of the AM radio station channel that will carry event traffic information, can be included in advance ticket-sales packets so that spectators are informed before they even leave their homes.

TRAFFIC MONITORING

Traffic monitoring should be carried out by periodic radio contact with ground personnel in the field of the event footprint and by surveillance from aerial observation platforms. Fixed-wing aircraft can stay airborne for extended periods of time to obtain the full view of traffic flow. Helicopters can be used to view both the full area and specific problem areas that may warrant closer attention than can be provided by fixed-wing aircraft. Stationary, closed-circuit TV cameras can also be considered for use in areas prone to congestion.

PUBLIC TRANSPORTATION

If public transportation is to be used by patrons for access to the event, a separate ticketing and admitting area can be established to permit smooth drop-off and pick-up. If available, public transportation should be encouraged by event organizers because it tends to lessen the negative impact on local community street traffic. It also decreases the number of parking attendants required at the event site. Another facet of public transportation for consideration is event-only transportation. At many large-scale events that require off-venue parking, promoters lease school or private buses to provide transportation from specific pick-up sites within the community and from remote event-specific parking areas. If public transportation is offered, planners must coordinate with law enforcement and public works personnel for assistance. Public works and law enforcement agencies may choose to close lanes or streets for use only by the public transportation vehicles.

TOWING AND DISABLED VEHICLES

Promoters should be required to hire towing companies to facilitate the removal of disabled or illegally parked vehicles. Tow trucks should be available and readily observable as private vehicles arrive at venue parking lots. The mere presence and active use of tow trucks can act as a deterrent for those motorists who may consider parking illegally. As a general rule, one tow truck for every 2,500 anticipated vehicles can be considered adequate for planning purposes. The size, type, and location of the event may change the needs.

Abandoned vehicles should be towed immediately, because these could be an indicator of a vehicle-borne improvised explosive device (VBIED), a current common tactic of terrorists.

Towing companies should establish a standard procedure for impounding and owner retrieval and should set maximum fees per impounded/towed vehicle in advance of the event. Also, a mechanism (database) for tracking where vehicles from certain areas have been towed and a mechanism for informing motorists of how to find their cars should be in place. (For example, establish a toll-free telephone number). This information should be shared with the appropriate authority and the command post, in case owners of towed vehicles arrive there to ask about their vehicles.

A consideration is for the promoter to be held accountable for any costs associated with towing that are not covered by towing fees. Public safety agencies should handle the regulation and oversight of any towing arrangements that are made during the planning process.

EVENT VEHICLE PRE-SCREENING

Some jurisdictions now screen vehicles at an event site days or weeks in advance of the event. For instance, it is common practice now for some State Fair venues to screen vendors and carnival vehicles upon their arrival.

PARKING

With the crowd and the traffic risks also come the inevitable parking problems. A basic formula for estimating parking requirements is to anticipate one vehicle for every three persons in attendance. Areas of specific concern are:

- Public parking arrangements—Have you made arrangements for overflow parking, signposting, and segregation of pedestrian and vehicular traffic? If spectator-parking areas overflow, will congestion on surrounding roads result?
- Parking control—If anticipated spectator parking areas become full, are there nearby areas for overflow parking? Are shuttle buses desirable, feasible, or necessary?
- Towing—Are towing policies established to determine where stalled or disabled vehicles will be towed, or how the owners can find their vehicles, and who bears the cost of towing and storage?

If parking is allowed adjacent to, or inside, the facility itself, vehicle screening should also be considered. Pre-event parking bans should also be considered to ensure the integrity of the footprint surrounding the event site. Sufficient posting of no-parking signs should be done in advance of the event and strictly enforced.

AUXILIARY PARKING LOTS/SHUTTLES

If the event venue does not have established parking lots available, then temporary, auxiliary lots need to be established. Considerations for these lots include:

- Lighting for hours of darkness
- Compliance with the ADA
- Publication of the location of the parking lots and the shuttles
- Provision of toilet facilities
- Use of public transportation (shuttle busses) to and from the event site

Assigning specific buses to specific lots helps the attendees as they go to and from the event. These lots should be clearly distinguished from one another and adequately marked. (Color-coding is one effective method of distinguishing buses. For example, Red Line buses, marked with a red dot in the window, go only to and from the red lot.) The location, of these lots need to be determined well in advance so that traffic management can evaluate them in relation to the overall incident traffic management plan. If the lots need to be rented or leased, the promoter should be held accountable by the permitting authority for any costs associated with their establishment.

Parking attendants in charge of the auxiliary lots are required to direct event spectators to park their cars in the configuration recommended by the traffic planner. If event spectators park their own cars, they may park in such a way that greatly diminishes the capacity of the parking lot, and control of traffic in and out of the lot can be lost. Parking attendants may be trained volunteers, paid promoter staff, or public safety personnel. A consideration is for the promoter to be held accountable for any costs associated with providing parking attendants.

PUBLIC HEALTH

Public health interventions are designed to prevent or minimize injury or ill health. Mass gatherings present particular challenges for preventing or at least minimizing, harm to participants, spectators, and event staff, especially when the event is held at a temporary venue. Familiarity of the financial stakeholders of the event with each other's roles and responsibilities, and knowledge of the potential and actual public health issues, present a common challenge.

This section provides guidance on the primary public health issues likely to arise during the planning phase of a mass gathering event. If State or local legislation is in place, that legislation takes precedence over advice contained in this manual.

PRE-EVENT PUBLIC HEALTH SURVEY

Event organizers should conduct a pre-event public health assessment for any venue intended for a mass spectator event. A Public Health Department Venue Assessment Checklist is included on pages A-47 and A-48 of Appendix A: Job Aids.

Organizers should consult appropriate health authorities to ascertain the availability of:

- Running water (particularly for hand washing by food service and medical personnel).
- Sufficient public toilets and hand washing stations in or adjacent to toilets (with provision for pump-out of portables and servicing as necessary during the event).
- Adequate refrigeration for perishable foodstuffs.
- Recognized, approved vendors of bulk food items delivered to the site's food providers.
- Sufficient number of covered containers for the storage of food and solid waste, including removal during the event.
- Appropriate storage and removal of liquid waste.

Public health inspectors should be available onsite during the event to monitor public health compliance.

Public health authorities onsite should have legislated authority to enforce "cease operation" orders on onsite food providers who are in contravention of standards or are otherwise operating contrary to the public interest.

PUBLIC HEALTH CONTINGENCY ARRANGEMENTS

The arrangements outlined in this chapter are designed to prevent an adverse event or minimize the risk that an adverse event will occur. However, unforeseen circumstances that may create a public health risk always exist. Some thought must be given to making contingency arrangements and documenting these arrangements in the public health emergency management plan. The plan should include the following details, as a minimum:

- Contact details, including after-hour information, for principal event personnel (for example, event organizers, environmental health officers, trades persons, and emergency service personnel, including health services personnel).
- Contact details for additional staff.
- Details for 24-hour contact of the food proprietors.
- Arrangements for alternative suppliers of equipment and utilities in the event of a failure or loss of water or power.
- Arrangements to replace food handlers who become ill.
- Arrangements in case of product recall.
- Epidemiological tracking procedures.
- Procedures for handling complaints.
- A debriefing procedure.

MONITORING HEALTH RISKS

First aid posts and security personnel can provide information to help assess health and safety risks. First aid posts can provide data by collecting gastrointestinal illness surveillance information. A Gastrointestinal Illness Questionnaire is included on pages A-60 and A-61 of Appendix A: Job Aids. First aid posts can also maintain records of injuries, incidents involving watercourses, and alcohol and drug issues. Security agencies can provide information on safety hazards and alcohol and drug issues.

FOOD SAFETY

Food safety is a vital element of public health planning for public events. Unless personnel apply proper sanitary practices to food storage, preparation, and distribution at mass gatherings, food may become contaminated and present a danger to public health. Special one-of-a-kind outdoor events that are held during warm weather pose additional risks because they tend to have less than ideal facilities for food handling, transport, and storage.

To ensure that adequate food safety standards are met and maintained, an environmental health officer should initially assess food service proposals, including the authorization of vendors, as part of the pre-event planning outlined in Chapter 1. The health officer should base any assessment on current local and State food hygiene legislation and food safety codes. The officer should follow this assessment with a pre-event audit as well as periodic monitoring of food safety throughout the event.

FOOD SAFETY (CONTINUED)

This assessment should form part of a comprehensive food safety plan for the event, including:

- Licensing/permit procedures and authorization of vendors
- Quantities and types of food
- Lines of supply
- Premises where food is stored
- Preparation techniques
- Disposal of foods
- Means of distribution
- Food safety documentation, approved approaches, and surveillance

Food vendors must meet appropriate licensing and registration requirements of the responsible health authority, including an off-premises food-catering license, as appropriate. During the event, onsite environmental health officers must have the authority to close down any vendor who is contravening food hygiene legislation and public health requirements. In some cases, this action may necessitate passing particular local laws or ordinances.

Appendix A includes a Food Vendor Information Sheet on pages A-33 through A-35. A Catering Inspection Checklist for Food Vendors is included on pages A-36 through A-39.

FOOD PREMISES

Setup and construction of the food premises must be in accordance with State and local regulations and codes of practice. The premises or areas to be used for food storage, preparation, and service must be easily cleaned and promote neither the harboring of rodents and insects nor the buildup of dirt and food particles.

EQUIPMENT

Equipment used in food preparation, distribution, and storage must be in safe working order and easily cleaned. Ensure that an appropriate number of the correct kind/type of fire extinguishers (e.g., effective for use with deep fryers, propane tanks, etc.) is available at food provider sites.

PERSONAL SAFETY

The safety of both staff and the public is always an important consideration, and you must meet occupational health and safety standards. Some of the hazards to avoid include loose power leads, trip hazards, inadequate refuse disposal, inappropriate positioning of equipment (especially hot equipment), poor ventilation and extreme temperatures in the work environment, badly stacked supplies, and unguarded equipment.

WASTE DISPOSAL

An effective disposal system should be put into place. Improper disposal of perishable goods, in particular, can cause problems arising from odor, insects or rodents, or other animals. Adequate disposal facilities must be easily accessible to food handlers and removal contractors.

Organize a separate refuse collection for food premises and continually monitor it to ensure that the frequency of collection is appropriate.

Where possible, encourage the separation of refuse into dry, wet, and hazardous disposal units. For more information on refuse disposal, refer to the discussion under Waste Management on page 2-31 of this chapter.

WATER SUPPLY

Provision of a supply of potable water for sinks is essential. Those operators who use water that is stored in their own tanks must have access to facilities to refill diminished supplies. Ensure that this access is established before the event. If possible, at outdoor concerts in extreme heat conditions, all potable water supply lines should be buried to avoid breakage and contamination by concert attendees. Having a NO GLASS policy is wise to prevent hazards caused by broken glass. For more specific details on water supply, refer to the section on Water on page 2-28 of this chapter.

HAND WASHING

Hand-washing facilities must be provided for the exclusive use of food handlers. Potable, running water must be used for hand washing, and, where possible, hot water should be available. Soap and disposable hand towels should be provided in the hand-washing area.

SINKS

Potable water must be supplied to all sink areas. Hot water should be used where possible. An appropriate detergent and sanitizer should be used to clean all sinks adequately.

FOOD SUPPLIES

Food should come only from registered outlets and should not be prepared in domestic kitchens. Food proprietors must ensure that food supplies have been prepared and transported in accordance with relevant standards.

TRANSPORTING FOOD

The time required for food transportation should be kept to a minimum. Temperature requirements should be maintained, and the food should be protected from contamination at all times.

Food transport vehicles should be clearly identified and subject to surveillance and monitoring.

FOOD HANDLING

Essential matters to address include the following:

Cross-Contamination—The following points apply:

- Every effort should be made to minimize the risk of cross-contamination during the food-handling process. Utensils and surfaces that are used for the preparation of either raw or ready-to-eat food should be clearly distinguished. In cramped circumstances, this distinction becomes more difficult to observe. Adequate cleaning and sanitizing of food utensils and surfaces between use plays an important role in reducing problems arising from cross-contamination.
- Disposable plastic gloves should be worn and changed frequently. The temptation to continue to wear the same gloves exists, even after the work being undertaken has changed. Encourage frequent hand washing.
- Appropriate food storage is critical to ensure that there is no contamination between raw and cooked or ready-to-eat foods. Raw foods should be stored separately if possible, or at a minimum, stored below cooked or ready-to-eat foods.
- Equipment must be adequately cleaned and sanitized after each separate process. This is particularly critical where equipment is used for preparing different types of food.

Thawing, Cooking, Heating, and Cooling—The goal in monitoring temperature control is to minimize the length of time during which potentially hazardous foods are held in temperatures between 41°F and 140°F. This is the temperature range in which most foodborne microorganisms can grow. This range is referred to as the danger zone. Key points to remember include:

- Thaw food under refrigeration or in cold, running water.
- Cook food thoroughly to applicable standards.
- Minimize the reheating of food. When reheating is required, heat the food thoroughly and store it appropriately.
- Cool food quickly under refrigeration.
- Apportion food into appropriately sized trays.

Cleaning and Sanitizing—The following points apply:

- Regardless of the type of facility in which the food is prepared, regularly clean and sanitize all food contact surfaces, using an appropriate sanitizer.
- Clean all other surfaces to minimize the risk of contamination of food products. Also be aware of pest infestation and occupational hazards, such as slippery floor surfaces. Adequate signage should be posted in these areas.
- Consider the provision of a designated wash-up area for food outlets to reduce sullage waste storage and pump out at each food outlet.

Chemical Storage—Store chemicals in areas separate from foods and clearly mark the contents on chemical storage containers. **Never use food containers to store chemicals**.

Food Storage

Essential matters to address include:

- Storage Facilities—Provide facilities of adequate size and appropriateness for the purpose.
- All foodstuffs must be stored off the floor or ground using shelving or pallets in accordance with State and local health regulations.
- Temperature Control—The following points apply:

  - Refrigerated or heated storage areas require a continuous power supply. You must store potentially hazardous food at appropriate temperatures at all times.
  - Refrigeration can pose a problem particularly in hot weather when refrigeration units struggle to cope. In case of refrigeration failure, all proprietors should indicate alternative refrigeration suppliers, or the organizer or authority could identify alternative suppliers in the public health emergency management plan.

- Cross-Contamination—The following problems must be overcome:

  - The less-than-ideal conditions that confront food handlers working in temporary facilities may lead to compromising appropriate food handling practices.
  - Space is often a major problem. Ensure that, at a minimum, raw and cooked or ready-to-eat-foods are stored appropriately. Food handling staff must be aware of the requirements for strict hand-washing procedures and for the cleaning and sanitizing of equipment between handling raw and ready-to-eat foods.

- Dry Goods—Appropriate and sufficient storage conditions should be available to ensure adequate protection of food from the elements and pests.
- Food Protection—Protect exposed food available on display from insect pests, dust, and human contact.

Food Handling Staff Considerations

Important matters to address include:

- Training—Encourage proprietors to select staff with food handler training to work in temporary facilities.
- Personal Hygiene—Selection of staff should include factors such as high personal hygiene standards. Food proprietors should ensure that a non-smoking policy is implemented in the workplace if permitted by local code.
- Communications—Proprietors should be able to demonstrate that they have an efficient reporting and communication system so that staff can identify public health problems and deal with them promptly.
- Supervision—Encourage proprietors to provide appropriate supervision to ensure a team approach to the provision of a safe food supply.
- Dress—Food handlers' dress should be appropriate to the tasks that they are performing and include some form of hair covering.
- Infectious Diseases—

  - Proprietors should be reminded that food handlers must not work while they are in an acute stage of any gastrointestinal illness or the common cold.
  - Proprietors should remind food handlers who have open wounds to dress all wounds with a waterproof dressing and to change the dressing regularly.
  - Provide segregated toilet facilities exclusively for food handlers.
  - Monitor these facilities for any signs of pest or rodent infestation.
  - Proprietors should keep a register of any complaints that they may receive from food purchasers.

HEALTH PROMOTION

Consider the opportunities to promote health messages at public events and to encourage event organizers and service providers, such as food vendors, to participate. Examples include:

Sunsmart—Encourage the provision and use of shade areas. Encourage the use of sunscreen creams and hats, and make them available for purchase by spectators. Organizers should consider advising spectators that alcohol consumption in the sun greatly increases the risk of dehydration. Additionally, organizers may want to consider providing "misting tents" which are used by attendees to reduce core body temperatures in excessive heat environments.

No Smoking—Encourage the provision of non-smoking areas and ban the sale of cigarettes at the event.

Alcohol—Consider the designation of alcohol-free areas or restrictions on the sale of alcohol. Also consider glass-free policies. Alcohol-free events will minimize aggressive behavior of spectators and also minimize the use of restrooms and water supply needs.

WATER

An adequate supply of safe drinking water must be available. One guideline suggests making available 21 quarts of potable water per person per day, of which 5 quarts comprise the drinking water component. Consider event duration and location and the anticipated ambient temperature in determining the quantity of potable water required.

All water provided must be tested to ensure its potability. In areas where non-reticulated water is the only source for personal use, then consider the clarification and disinfecting of the water supply to achieve a level greater than 1 ppm residual chlorine.

Some consideration must be made to ensure that the water is safe from deliberate contamination. Placing the water supply in a secure area or having someone guard the water supply are two options available.

Appropriate access to drinking water must be available for spectators in a field or outdoor venue or at events such as "raves," where the activity produces an extreme-heat environment.

Water pressure must be adequate to provide for all normal use and for use during peak demands. Any use of fire-suppression water systems (i.e., fire hydrants) should be discouraged, or alternate water supplies must be made available in case existing supplies fail to meet demand or if the supply is rendered unsafe or unusable.

TOILETS

Where existing toilet facilities are judged inadequate, you must make available additional portable units.

Toilet locations should be:

- Well marked.
- Near hand-washing stations.
- Well lit (including the surrounding area) if night use is anticipated.
- Serviced (including pump-out of portables) on a 24-hour schedule during the event (Vehicle access is obviously necessary).
- Located away from food storage and food service areas.
- Secured to prevent tipping.

The following considerations will determine the number of toilets to be provided for particular events:

- Duration of the event
- Type of crowd
- Weather conditions
- Whether the event is pre-ticketed with the numbers of attendees known, or unticketed
- Whether finishing times are staggered if the event has multi-functions
- Whether alcohol will be consumed

TOILETS (CONTINUED)

Calculating the number of toilets required for an event can be a particular challenge. Where local laws or regulations do not exist, the following guidelines can be applied. Better management of events can be achieved by providing additional facilities. Assume a 50/50 male/female split unless otherwise advised. The following tables should be used only as a guide.

Toilet facilities for events where alcohol is not available

Patrons	Males			Females	
	Toilets	Urinals	Sinks	Toilets	Sinks
<500	1	2	2	6	2
<1,000	2	4	4	9	4
<2,000	4	8	6	12	6
<3,000	6	15	10	18	10
<5,000	8	25	17	30	17

Toilet facilities for events where alcohol is available

Patrons	Males			Females	
	Toilets	Urinals	Sinks	Toilets	Sinks
<500	3	8	2	13	2
<1,000	5	10	4	16	4
<2,000	9	15	7	18	7
<3,000	10	20	14	22	14
<5,000	12	30	20	40	20

These figures may be reduced for shorter duration events as follows:

Duration of event	Quantity required
More than 8 hours	100%
6-8 hours	80%
4-6 hours	75%
Less than 4 hours	70%

Toilets for the Disabled

At least one unisex toilet for the disabled is required. Check with your local ADA office for further guidance.

Food Vendors' Toilets

Separate toilet and hand-washing facilities should be made available for food handlers.

General Considerations

In an outdoor setting, it is a relatively simple matter to provide additional toilets by contracting for temporary portable toilets. This solution may not be suitable for indoor settings, for which provision of additional toilets may be more difficult. One possible solution is to convert some men's washrooms to women's facilities for events where you anticipate a predominantly female audience, or vice versa.

To avoid long lines, particularly at female toilets, organizers may identify some toilet facilities as unisex toilets.

The maintenance and cleaning schedule for toilets and sinks should ensure:

- An adequate supply of toilet paper and soap.
- Clean toilets throughout the duration of the event.
- Provision for disposal and removal of sanitary napkins.
- Availability of a plumber or appropriate maintenance person to repair or remove blockages.

Organizers should ensure that adequate cleaning supplies are available for use by the cleaning staff.

SHOWERS

At an extended event, promoters and planners may decide to provide showers. If they do provide showers, they must consider the additional demands for potable water and drainage. If municipal water supplies and wastewater treatment plants cannot service the shower facilities, providing shower facilities could prove to be a very costly and formidable task. Vendors are available that will contract to provide self-contained shower units. Ensure that showers are located on high ground so that muddy areas are not created.

SOLID AND LIQUID WASTE MANAGEMENT

Major considerations are as follows:

FOOD WASTE

- Deposit food waste in covered containers placed strategically around the venue. Covers are essential, especially in outdoor settings or if high temperatures are expected.
- Spectator density may prohibit access by garbage removal vehicles. To prevent containers from overflowing, empty containers regularly and move waste to a temporary, properly prepared holding area until bulk removal can be accomplished at designated times or after the event. Removing food waste often and in a timely manner prevents disease and pests.

EMPTY CONTAINERS

Make arrangements for the appropriate storage or disposal of empty containers, such as cardboard boxes.

HAZARDOUS WASTES

Special arrangements must be established for the collection and disposal of various forms of hazardous waste, including waste from food preparation areas, medical sharps, and other hazardous materials.

CLINICAL WASTE

Ensure there is provision for the storage, collection, and disposal of clinical waste generated from onsite medical and first aid facilities.

SEWAGE AND SULLAGE

Provide and maintain adequate facilities for the ongoing storage and disposal of sewage and sullage. As with all other wastes, these must be removed in a timely manner and on a frequent basis.

RECYCLING

Where possible, consider providing specific containers for recyclable materials. Vendors should be encouraged to use recyclable packaging of foodstuffs. A sufficient number of dedicated containers should be placed near the vendor area to further encourage recycling.

ANIMALS, RODENTS, AND VEGETATION

In outdoor settings, the control of rodents, spiders, mosquitoes, and insects of significance to public health must be addressed. Venue sites should also be inspected for pests, snakes, gopher holes, etc., in advance. If particular hazardous species are known to inhabit the area, or if carriers of particular diseases are prevalent in the area, alert the attending first aid and medical personnel.

Alert medical and first aid personnel to the presence of potentially poisonous and noxious plants and trees in the area.

If domestic animals are permitted into the venue, establish rules for the control of animals and their waste. Check with your local animal control agency or shelter for more guidance concerning animal regulations.

Also consider the potential effect of the event on nearby domestic or farm animals and native fauna.

SWIMMING AND WATER SAFETY

Purpose-built swimming areas must comply with State requirements for water quality and meet other local requirements, such as fencing. Assess the suitability of other watercourses in the vicinity of the venue if spectators may use those watercourses for water recreation or washing. If these watercourses do not meet requirements, fence them off and erect warning signs against their use.

Address water quality in both designated swimming areas and areas that could be used for swimming in hot weather. Experience has shown that where audiences attend an outdoor concert in hot weather, particularly in overnight events without adequate or convenient washing facilities, they will employ any nearby water area as a makeshift swimming, bathing, or washing area.

Consider making available some form of trained supervision for:

- Families with small children.
- Spectator groups for which alcohol consumption, with subsequent judgment impairment, is anticipated.
- Areas of water that pose additional hazards such as steep, slippery sides; submerged snags; or unusually variable depths.

INFECTION CONTROL AND PERSONAL HYGIENE CONCERNS

Infectious disease transmission through unsafe sexual practices or drug use may be a health risk at some events, particularly for those at which spectators are camping at the venue overnight. To reduce these risks, consider providing or making available condoms and a properly licensed needle exchange/disposal mechanism. While these are sensitive and controversial issues, and political issues in some areas, they are nevertheless important public health concerns in contemporary society, and you should address them.

At events where the duration extends overnight or longer, provide hygienic washing facilities. Suggested minimum requirements for facilities at campgrounds, based on two to three nights' camping, are as follows:

Sex	Toilets	Urinal	Sinks	Shower
M	1 per 50	1 per 100	1 per 75	1 per 100
F	1 per 25	N/A	1 per 75	1 per 100

TATTOOING AND BODY PIERCING

With a return in popularity of tattoos, body piercing, and branding, mobile operators have begun to appear at certain types of public gatherings, such as carnivals, motorcycle races, and auto swap meets. Where this activity is likely to occur, check the need for proper licensing or registration of such service providers and their compliance with any health legislation.

Because of the potential of cross-infection, particularly of blood-borne diseases, inspect any such operations to ensure, as a minimum, the use of:

- Disposable, single-use skin penetration items.
- Proper sterilization equipment and techniques.
- Clinical sharps containers for used needle disposal.
- Sharps containers safely located away from children.
- Safe disposal of used sharps containers.

If the service providers do not use these minimum infection control procedures, do not allow them to perform any skin penetration procedures.

POST-EVENT PUBLIC HEALTH SURVEY

Conduct a post-event survey to ensure that personnel have conducted a proper cleanup, particularly from a public health perspective. For example, check that all scrap foodstuffs and discarded needles are properly disposed of. All involved in planning the event should return the venue to its pre-event condition.

As an additional precaution, retain appropriate records of all service providers at the event so that they may be traced if a subsequent outbreak of a reportable disease occurs or if a claim is made for an injury or illness.

Health personnel should also be conscious of the need to introduce a monitoring or surveillance system if they subsequently become aware of any particular health problem arising from an event.

A formal public health debriefing should follow the event, and a public health representative should participate in all agency debriefings.

MEDICAL CARE

Spectators and participants at mass gatherings may require medical attention in the event of illness or injury. The incidence of illness will be greater at an event for spectators than that expected to occur naturally in a population of comparable size.

The number of spectators who require, or avail themselves of, onsite medical care, and the types of problems that they present, will vary significantly depending on the nature of the event. Generally, between 0.3 percent to 1.3 percent[4] of event attendees will require some form of medical assistance, regardless of the character, locale, physical layout, and size of the event.

Alcohol and drug use is common at most festivals and is the primary diagnosis in more than 10 per cent of the persons seeking medical care. Other common complaints include lacerations, fractures and sprains, burns, sunburn, heat stroke, seizures, asthma, and exposure.

MEDICAL CARE PROVISION

Planning for the provision of medical care for both spectators and participants is essential, for both humanitarian and legal reasons. The permitting process should ensure that medical care at the venue is equal to or greater than the standard of care currently provided in the community. In addition, providing onsite first aid or medical care will significantly reduce the demand on EMS and the emergency departments at local hospitals in the area of the event.

---

[4] Leonard, Ralph B., PhD, MD, FACEP & Moreland, Kimberly M., MD, *"EMS for the Masses, Preplanning Your EMS Response To a Major Event,"* EMS, January 2001.

MEDICAL CARE PROVISION (CONTINUED)

Event organizers may choose to contract with a health service provider, who may not be associated with the usual local service provider. Check to ensure that the service provider is appropriately licensed and regulated. The provider must coordinate with the local health and emergency services to plan a response to any emergency or significant medical problems requiring further assistance. Notify local health authorities of the details of the event and provide them with emergency plans for a major incident. Additionally, local hospitals should be notified of the event in writing at least 30 days in advance and given the estimated number of attendees.

MAIN CONCERNS IN PLANNING MEDICAL CARE

Main issues to address in medical care planning include:

LOGISTICS

Some medical logistics questions to consider in planning an event include:

- How many medical stations will be required onsite?
- Will medical personnel operate in a facility to which the injured must make their way, or will clearly identified medical teams patrol spectator areas?
- How will spectators identify medical personnel on the site (uniforms, vests, etc.)?
- Will vehicles be available to transport spectators to the medical facility?
- Will medical vehicles be appropriate to the terrain? Four-wheel-drive vehicles may be required for off-road areas and golf carts or similar vehicles required for high-density spectator areas.
- Where an ambulance is not required, will a "chauffeur system" be provided to transport persons from the onsite medical facility to their own transport vehicle?
- How will medical personnel be notified of, or summoned to, spectators requiring assistance in vast spectator areas?
- What means of communication will be available to permit attending medical personnel to communicate with offsite medical personnel, event organizers, security, and other support personnel?
- Are there any sponsorship conflicts between the event sponsor and any medical service operators?
- What level of onsite medical care, if any, do you expect to be required, given the nature of the event?
- What mix of medical personnel (first aid providers, paramedics, nurses, doctors) will you require onsite?
- Who will provide the personnel? How will the cost for their services be funded?
- Are the health service providers from the local area? If not, how will their services be integrated with the local services?
- How will security concerns for health care personnel onsite be addressed?
- Are the selected personnel appropriately skilled to respond to anticipated medical problems at the event? They may require additional training.
- Will medical personnel or vehicles need special credentials to allow them access to all parts of the venue, especially to any restricted areas?
- Are medical personnel assigned for public safety workers at the event?

LOGISTICS (CONTINUED)

- Are aero-medical services and landing zones available?
- Where is the closest trauma center?
- Have primary and secondary receiving hospitals been identified?
- Does the area hospital have adequate bed and personnel capacity to respond to the emergency requirements of an event of the size that is being planned?

Management and Planning

- Determine which other organizations will be involved. Who will be the lead agency?
- Conduct planning meetings involving health personnel, emergency services personnel, and event organizers.
- Determine what is expected of each organization involved in the provision of medical care.
- Determine likely levels of care that will be required.
- Determine any local laws, rules, or regulations governing emergency first aid.
- Determine the budget for the provision of medical care services.
- Establish liaison with other emergency services (police, fire, and security).
- Identify the equipment required and potential suppliers. Will the equipment be purchased, hired, or borrowed?
- Will volunteers be used? What accreditation will they be required to possess? What benefits will they be offered?
- Ensure the security of medical stations and the safety of the staff.
- Establish a patient information management system for patients who are treated, including patient care reporting, etc.
- Determine in advance the disposition of patient records after the event.

An Emergency Medical Services Venue Assessment Checklist is included on pages A-53 and A-54 of Appendix A: Job Aids.

PLANNING INFORMATION

Obtain background information to assist with medical care planning that may be available from:

- Reports from previous similar events (medical and other specialist literature).
- Lay literature (press).
- Medical literature that has information on the risks and types of injury that were sustained at similar events in the past.

Consider the effects of weather conditions on the spectators, such as hypothermia and heat stroke.

Consult medical literature for information on the numbers of casualties from similar events in the past. See the table below for anticipated percentages of patients against triage categories. Consider variables that affect numbers (for example, alcohol consumption, psychosocial behavior, and type of event).

PLANNING INFORMATION (CONTINUED)

Expected percentages of patients in triage categories

Categories [1]	Description	Vital Signs	Mental State	Percentage[2]
1	Critical	Unstable	Abnormal	0.02
2	Serious	Potentially Unstable	Potentially Abnormal	1.1
3	Moderate	Usually Stable	Normal	12
4	Minor	Stable	Normal	87

Notes: [1] Categories modified from disaster triage guidelines.
[2] Percentages aggregated from events listed in the references.

CASUALTIES

Experience from other events has shown that most casualties are from:

- Heat stroke, dehydration.
- Cuts from broken glass and drink can ring pulls.
- Injuries from missiles, usually bottles and cans.
- Fainting and exhaustion from a combination of hysteria, heat and alcohol. At concerts, this often occurs at or near the stage barrier.
- Trampling or crushing from crowd pressure.
- Crowd "surfing" and stage diving.
- Illicit drug and alcohol abuse.
- Respiratory problems (asthma and emphysema).
- Epilepsy attacks brought about from strobe lighting.
- Age-related illness.

MEDICAL ACCESS TO VENUE

Consider the risks associated with venue (for example, water in the vicinity).

Agreements must be reached among medical service providers on the following:

- Medical teams must be able to locate individuals in need of attention easily. You should agree on the use of a common reference map or grid system.
- How will medical teams reach or rescue individuals in distress for example, in crowded areas or through fixed seating)?
- How will patients be transported onsite?
- Will you provide a dedicated access route, or emergency service lane, to allow rapid access to and from the venue for ambulances and other emergency vehicles?
- Will the event itself pose a barrier to medical teams (for example, community runs or a parade)?
- Will you need aero-medical services/landing zones, and if so, what are the associated regulations regarding their operation?

MEDICAL REQUIREMENTS

- Prepare for the most critical injury or illness foreseeable, such as cardiac arrest.
- Is there a need for a mobile team? This team may require pre-packed medical kits.
- Determine who will provide care for the audience, any VIPs, and performers.
- Define boundaries of care (for example, inside the venue and in the parking areas).

LEVEL OF CARE

Levels of care can be categorized as follows:

- <u>Basic</u>—first aid.
- <u>Intermediate</u>—first aid plus IV therapy and oxygen.
- <u>Advanced</u>—Care and life support and early management of severe trauma.
- <u>Site Hospital</u>—full monitoring, ventilation, and resuscitation capability.

Other level-of-care concerns include:

- Consulting medical personnel with experience in similar events to determine the appropriate levels of care to provide.
- Considering the distance to, and accessibility of, the nearest hospital and its capability.
- Pre-establishing the coordination between venue medical services and those of the local community emergency medical service responders (that is, establish how they will provide mutual aid if required).
- Preparing to treat patients after a release of a chemical, biological, radiological or other CBRNE material.

Further guidance on the establishment of medical care facilities and their equipment requirements is available in the references and from local or regional disaster and health plans.

MEDICAL TEAMS

When deploying medical teams, consider the following:

- What will be the size of the event?
- What is the location of the venue with regard to medical infrastructure?
- What is the extent of available medical resources?
- How do local and State ordinances and regulations apply, including those that may address minimum staffing levels? Average numbers of expected patients generally range from .3 percent to 1.3 percent of the total number of patrons in attendance[5].
- Who can see, treat, and discharge patients?
- Will there be peak periods or special circumstances requiring additional staff?
- How will medical staff be fed, watered, rested, and protected from the elements?
- Are work safety regulations established that cover occupational health and safety (for example, protection from violence and crowd crushes)?
- Have medical teams been provided with maps of the venue?
- What arrangements are in place for movement of medical teams onto and off the site?
- Are medical team members appropriately dressed for the conditions?
- Is the dress of medical team members easily identifiable?
- Are interpreters required?
- Do medical teams understand the command structure and their role within it, and the emergency activation system?
- Have medical personnel been trained and equipped with PPE for use in response to a CBRNE incident.

MOBILE TEAMS

In tightly packed areas, particularly near the stage, first aid personnel on foot, bicycles, or golf carts may have the only access. Experience has shown that uniformed first aid personnel on foot circulating in dense spectator areas are quite effective, and patrons will readily summon them in an emergency, even if the person requiring care is a stranger to them. Even if a clearly marked field hospital is visible, spectators are often unwilling to make the sometimes long trek to request assistance (because they may lose their seating position), particularly for a fellow spectator whom they may not know or if they fail to appreciate the seriousness of the patient's condition.

Identification of mobile teams, where ambulance or clinical uniforms are unsuitable, can be successfully accomplished by special event uniforms. Mobile teams need to have communications equipment to keep EMS supervisors and the Incident Command Post informed at all times.

(**NOTE**: The Red Cross symbol is registered by the International Red Cross and its National Societies. It should not be used as part of an event uniform.)

---

[5] Leonard, Ralph B., PhD, MD, FACEP & Moreland, Kimberly M., MD, *"EMS for the Masses, Preplanning Your EMS Response To a Major Event,"* EMS, January 2001.

MEDICAL AID POSTS

Important considerations in the establishment of medical aid posts require that they should:

- Provide easy ambulance access and egress.
- Be located within 5 minutes of all sections of the crowd.
- Have available a mode of transport to them.
- Be clearly marked.
- Have adequate signage for direction to the aid post.
- Be clearly identified.
- Be clearly marked on maps of the venue layout.
- Be in a position known by security and other event personnel.
- Be stocked and staffed for the duration of the event and for spectator arrival and departure periods.
- Provide facilities for injured or sick patients to lie down.
- Ensure privacy in clinical areas.
- Provide some means of communication with the primary medical control point, venue control, and with mobile medical teams in the venue.
- Be located in as quiet a place as possible.
- Ensure that post security staff considerations are addressed.
- Include dedicated disposal containers for ablutions, hazardous wastes, and sharps.

GUIDE TO THE PROVISION OF MEDICAL AID

The number of medical aid personnel and posts will vary with the type of event. As a guide, use the following formulation:

Patrons	Medical Aid Personnel	Medical Aid Posts
500	2	1
1,000	4	1
2,000	6	1
5,000	8	2
10,000	12	2
20,000	22+	4

The number of medical aid posts required would depend on what medical aid room facilities are available. Every venue should have at least one climate-controlled facility with electrical service and running potable water.

Medical aid providers are generally not required for events that are smaller than 500 patrons and are held in close proximity to central ambulance/hospital services.

SITE HOSPITAL

Depending on the nature of the event, a site or field hospital may be needed to provide resuscitation or care for the number of casualties anticipated. You should also make contingency plans in case of a major incident, for which the resources of the field hospital may not be sufficient. Failure to plan for large numbers of casualties or severely injured patrons can result in long delays in providing medical treatment. It is important to provide a communication link between the site hospital and local hospitals.

Site hospitals will require:

- Clean water.
- Electricity for medical appliances and adequate lighting in tent hospitals at night. (This installation should, if possible, include a backup power system.)
- Washroom/rest facilities for the exclusive use of staff and patients.
- Provisions for patient modesty/privacy issues.
- Meals for medical staff.
- Tents for hospital use that have flooring as part of the structure to contain the service and to prevent ingress of water or insects.
- A landline telephone service for ordering additional staff or supplies and for notifying hospitals of patient transfers. (Note that cellular telephones should be used as backup devices only).
- Reserved access roads for emergency vehicle use.
- Dedicated disposal containers for ablutions, hazardous wastes, and sharps.

DOCUMENTATION

Documentation should facilitate:

- Post-event review of medical assistance activities.
- Tracking of biological, chemical, and infectious disease exposures, if they occur.

Medical and legal issues, which must be addressed prior to the preparation of any documents, are as follows:

- Who has access to records?
- Who keeps the data and for how long?
- Who can give consent for treatment?
- Health Insurance Portability and Accountability Act (HIPAA) considerations (i.e., privacy).

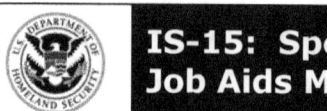

AMBULANCE VEHICLES

Organizers should consult ambulance services to determine ambulance requirements for the event. Some considerations include:

- Will ambulances be pre-positioned onsite or be called to the venue on an as-required basis?
- Has the security of the vehicles when parked been addressed?
- Are there provisions for a mix of Advanced and Basic Life Saving ambulances at the event?
- If ambulances are onsite specifically for athletes, race car drivers, etc., are these ambulances exclusively for taking care of their needs or emergencies, or will they be available for injured spectators as well?
- Is there a need for dedicated ambulances/medical staff for the event staff itself?
- Are aero-medical services/landing zones available? Who will pay for the service? Can the promoter be required to provide the service?

While conventional ambulances are appropriate for patient transfers to offsite medical facilities over good roads, such vehicles may be unsuitable for off-road use. Ad hoc roadways and cross-country terrain may require four-wheel-drive vehicles, particularly if grounds are saturated by recent rainfall. Because four-wheel-drive ambulances are not available in most areas, other four-wheel-drive vehicles, equipped with appropriate medical equipment (including, but not limited to, resuscitation equipment, trauma kit, and spinal board) can serve as ambulances over the short distances between spectator areas and medical care facilities.

In denser spectator areas, any vehicle can have access problems. You should consider using golf carts, either designed or modified to accommodate a litter or stretcher.

For these reasons the ambulance network may have to consist of a mix of first aid personnel on foot, golf-carts, four-wheel-drive vehicles, ambulance buses, and conventional ambulances, to facilitate patient transport requirements. You should provide a magnetic-based beacon, portable radio, and appropriate marking for these vehicles.

A communications network, designed to provide a coordinated response to requests for assistance, is essential. You may base the network on existing service networks, or event organizers may need to provide the network.

MEDICAL EQUIPMENT

The requirement for basic or advanced life support equipment depends on the type of event and the assessed risk of illness or injury. While standard lists of equipment will cover most requirements, you should review literature, previous experiences, and current practices.

Further equipment considerations include:

- Mobile versus fixed requirements.
- Arrangements to re-supply aid posts as required.
- Compatibility of onsite equipment with equipment used by ambulance and other health care providers (e.g., IV tubing/administration sets).
- Ambulance providers may want to consider carrying extra supplies beyond their normal supply.
- Provisions for the rapid movement of reserve supplies in a mass casualty incident should also be considered.

OTHER MEDICAL CONSIDERATIONS

Further considerations include:

- Providing considerations for interviewing and treating of sexual assault victims and the collection of evidence.
- Ensuring sufficient water supplies.
- Providing sprinkler systems or misting tents for crowds in hot, open areas, if they are suitable for the event.
- Providing welfare and information services (the helping and caring role).
- Assisting with forgotten medications.
- Providing a baby diaper-changing and caring facility.
- Containing and disposing of clinical waste.
- Determining how, and by whom, medical supplies will be obtained, including secure onsite storage of drugs.
- Planning for the deployment or availability of chemical antidote supplies (i.e., Mark 1 Kits, atropine, pediatric auto injectors) for a CBRNE event.

ENVIRONMENTAL CONCERNS

WEATHER

Weather is a variable that takes on a different significance depending on the event and its location. For a major indoor event in a southern United States city, weather is seldom a major concern, unless a natural disaster, such as a hurricane, is anticipated. If you were to move that same event to a northern United States climate in February, you would be faced with additional concerns, sometimes even for a predicted "normal" winter storm. Slow-moving traffic patterns, snow removal in parking areas, and safe movement of spectators from parking areas to the venue are a few concerns. Extreme high and low temperatures must be part of the contingency planning for an event. These extremes present hazards and risks that are not normally present but must be considered in the event that they do occur.

For outdoor events, many additional concerns may become apparent regardless of location. Lightning strikes, severe thunderstorms and hail, high winds, and other undesirable weather pose threats to event patrons. The influx of patrons may have a severe negative impact on the jurisdiction's mass evacuation and sheltering plan for local residents. Contingency plans drawn up for the jurisdiction may not provide for a transient population (as in the case of some rock concerts with numbers of patrons in the hundreds of thousands) that will negatively impact that community's ability to protect residents and visitors.

During the planning phase, event organizers must adequately consider all potential weather conditions. For example, if event infrastructure (i.e., stages, speaker towers, etc.) are to be erected at the event, special consideration should be given to their composition (i.e., steel versus wood, etc.), height, location, and protection of their surrounding areas. Electrical professionals can be consulted regarding the impact of a lightning strike scenario to this type of infrastructure by a swift-moving thunderstorm. Worst-case scenarios can then be developed to consider the effect of infrastructure energized by a lightning strike. Not only could anyone on the stage or scaffolding be prone to electrocution, but many spectators on the ground around the infrastructure could be in danger, depending on the location of the strike with the scaffolding, any grounding mechanisms in place, and the severity of the storm.

Some planning considerations involving weather awareness are:

- Monitoring the weather using a computer, radio, NOAA weather radio, or television.
- Establishing a dedicated a phone line that is linked with the closest office of the National Weather Service.
- Ensuring that ICS team consults with the Weather Service on a regular basis and that consultation information is included in each Operational Period's Incident Action Plan.
- Distributing weather information to the participants.
- Contracting or partnering with a private-sector meteorological prediction service.
- Establishing agreements with the promoter to interrupt a performance and use the festival sound equipment as a public-address system to give information to patrons on protective actions to take if severe weather becomes imminent.
- Coordinating with the Red Cross and concert organizers to designate specific buildings as evacuation shelters if the visiting public requires sheltering.
- Leasing and installing a lightning detection system similar to those used at major golfing events to forewarn of impending storms.

Weather (Continued)

Developing severe-weather contingency plans to ensure the safety of event attendees can require a significant amount of time, equipment, planning, and multi-agency participation.

Site Hazards

In selecting a site, especially for an outdoor event, the planning team should identify the potential hazards in the area, which include:

- Power lines that could be brought down by a severe storm.
- Structures and equipment that could be prone to lightning strikes.
- Waterways that may be prone to flooding.
- Brushfires.
- High winds.
- Areas of high ground that require management (i.e., security from snipers, etc.).
- Extremes of temperature.
- Pests and large animals, including:

  - Rodents
  - Insects—ants, caterpillars, wasps, bees, mosquitoes, flies
  - Snakes
  - Spiders

- Pollens and poisonous plants, including noxious weeds.
- Marshes or swamps.
- Quarries, pits.
- Scrap piles.
- Cliffs and steep inclines.
- Watercourses, including their depth of water, water currents, water temperature, water clarity.
- Pollution—dust, noise (including the potential need for hearing protection).
- Water quality (bacteriological), blue-green algae.
- Darkness.
- Hazardous chemicals or underground tanks.
- Use of lasers.
- Alcohol, drugs, weapons, or potential weapons (for example, broken glass).
- Ultraviolet (UV) radiation.
- Neighboring land use.

ENVIRONMENTAL IMPACT CONCERNS/MAINTAINING COMPLIANCE

To ensure compliance with public health requirements, carry out a public health audit just prior to the commencement of the event. Also undertake subsequent periodic surveillance during the event. These procedures are particularly important for outdoor events in hot weather with transient food vendors who may not have sufficient sanitary or refrigeration mechanisms available to meet established public health or safety protocols.

Environmental health officers should have access to resources to assist in early intervention and problem correction and resolution when any problem is noted (for example, toilet servicing, unsafe areas, fencing repairs, water testing) rather than using their authority to stop the event or particular operation.

AIRCRAFT

If helicopter flights will be available for spectators or members of the media to view the event from the air, the following concerns should be addressed:

- Will flights be prohibited directly over the event and spectators and confined, instead, to circular paths around the perimeter?
- Will helispots be confined to the periphery of the event, to avoid flights directly above spectators during take-offs and landings?
- Do the proposed helispots comply with Federal regulations governing such use?
- Which public safety agency working the event will be designated as responsible for interacting with the Federal Aviation Administration (FAA) if required?

CAMPING

If camping is permitted at the event, you should consider the following:

- Providing for the safety of the campers and their belongings.
- Disposing of solid and liquid waste.
- Clearly marking temporary streets.
- Clearly defining avenues of access for ambulances, law enforcement personnel, and other emergency vehicles.
- Controlling the building of fires.
- Removing fire hazards ahead of time.
- Installing a public address system to communicate emergencies to campers.

Survey proposed camping areas to ascertain their safety, paying particular attention to:

- Low-lying areas subject to flooding.
- Areas adjacent to creeks or rivers.
- Areas near utility lines.
- Trees that may drop branches, especially during a severe storm.

HAZARDOUS MATERIALS (HAZMAT)

The nature of some events causes concerns about hazardous materials (e.g., propane gas cylinders used for cooking, pyrotechnic lighting areas, oxygen tanks used by EMS, etc.) and the ability of local officials to handle HazMat incidents. In most communities, the fire department is the agency that responds to calls. The best way to plan for the handling of hazardous materials is to inform the fire department ahead of time about potential hazards and their locations. Providing fire officials with an event footprint grid map with a description of the possible hazards reduces the response time and allows the responding agency to be prepared. If the local fire company is not adequately trained or equipped to handle the hazardous material, planners must identify in advance the closest department that is equipped and consider staging them nearby during the event.

CYLINDER ANCHORAGE

At many public events, portable pressurized gas cylinders are used to inflate children's balloons, to carbonate beverages, or to provide cooking fuel. Frequently, such cylinders are not secured, or are merely fastened to two-wheeled hand trolleys designed to transport them, which are themselves not independently secured.

If such cylinders topple and the cylinder neck or valve cracks, the uncontrolled release of the stored pressurized gas can turn the cylinder into a deadly projectile. For this reason, all portable gas cylinders must be secured.

Used incorrectly, propane can be deadly. Propane is a flammable material that is heavier than air that is used for cooking at many large events. Tanks must be properly secured. Qualified inspectors, usually from the fire service, should also make periodic inspections of the tanks to ensure that the location is a safe distance away from heat sources or other possible sources of danger.

CHEMICAL, BIOLOGICAL, RADIOLOGICAL, NUCLEAR, EXPLOSIVE (CBRNE)

The CBRNE threat of weapons of mass destruction (WMD) is currently a much-discussed topic in this country. The Federal Government is prepared to assist communities in the event of a terrorist attack. The local community's first responders will be the first line of defense, but if the attack is beyond their capability, they may seek assistance from the State or Federal Government.

The Department of Defense has created WMD Civil Support Teams (CST) to assist the FBI and local communities facing a terrorist attack. These teams are made up of National Guard members who assist in the detection and identification of WMDs. Because these teams are composed of National Guard personnel, State Governors also may deploy these teams to assist communities.

A HazMat/CBRNE Data Collection Report is included on pages A-82 through A-84 of Appendix A: Job Aids.

A Weapon of Mass Destruction (WMD) is defined as:

- Any weapon that is designed or intended to cause death or serious bodily injury through the release, dissemination, or impact of toxic or poisonous chemicals, or their precursors.
- Any weapons involving a disease organism.
- Any weapon that is designed to release radiation or radioactivity at a level dangerous to human life.

Other terms associated with WMDs are:

SECONDARY DEVICE

A secondary device is usually explosive and designed to injure first responders when they arrive at an incident. Following the arrival of the first responders, a second device explodes in the responder area. A secondary device was recently used at an abortion clinic explosion.

ANTI-PERSONNEL DEVICES

Anti-personnel devices are used to injure people and may or may not be considered secondary devices that target responders.

SPECIFIC THREAT

A specific threat explains what will occur, for example, "A bomb will go off in one hour in the parking garage."

NON-SPECIFIC THREAT

A non-specific threat does not explain what may occur, for example, "Everyone in the building is going to die."

CAPABILITY

Capability refers to credible information that a specific group possesses the requisite training, skills, financial means, and access to the resources that are necessary to develop, produce, or acquire a particular type of WMD in a quantity or potency sufficient to produce mass casualties, combined with information substantiating the group's ability to safely store, test, and deliver the weapon.

CHEMICAL

Chemicals may be used as weapons or to deliver an attack. Originally, the military designed chemical weapons to use in wartime. The results of chemicals used as weapons were so devastating in warfare that many countries rejected their future use and created treaties to forbid their future use and manufacture. In 1995, terrorists attacked a Tokyo subway. Twelve persons died, 4,500 were injured, and more than 700 required extended hospital stays. The ease of access to chemical agents and the amount of damage they cause make chemical warfare very appealing to radical groups. Directions for the creation and use of chemical weapons can be found on the Internet.

Chemical agents include nerve agents, blood agents, choking agents, and blister agents. These agents create a credible threat for use by terrorists, and there is a high probability that chemical agents are likely to be encountered by this country in the future.

Responders must be prepared to manage a terrorist attack involving a chemical agent. To prepare, they should become knowledgeable of the range of chemical agents used by terrorists in the recent past. Knowledge of chemicals and their effects assists in the first stages of treatment. Each community should establish chemical weapons attack response plans and review them regularly. There is Federal training available to train responders in chemical agent response.

BIOLOGICAL

Biological terrorism is not a new type of warfare. Biological agents are by far the most dangerous of the three types of weapons of mass destruction. Agents include bacteria, fungi, viruses, and toxins that induce disease or death in any living thing.

The difficulty in countering biological terrorism begins with identifying it. Another serious concern arising from the use of all biological agents is the time that can elapse before their use by terrorists is discovered. Biological attacks can be slow acting, with the symptoms not appearing until as many as 21 days after exposure. The further contamination of additional population by those initially exposed multiplies exponentially as the time from the initial exposure increases. The best defense against the spread of the biological element is accurate documentation and tracking of this kind of WMD by medical personnel to contain the exposure.

With many countries facing economic difficulties at the end of the Cold War, experts fear that they may have sold their biological weapons to the highest bidder. However, the lack of an effective delivery system to deploy a biological agent currently limits the ability for widespread impact upon the population.

RADIOLOGICAL

Radiological agents are materials that emit ionizing radiation that could be dispersed into the environment using devices such as an explosive or other dispersal device.

A radiation threat, commonly referred to as a "dirty bomb" or "radiological dispersion device (RDD)", is the use of common explosives to spread radioactive materials over a targeted area. It is not a nuclear blast. The force of the explosion and radioactive contamination will be more localized. While the blast will be immediately obvious, the presence of radiation will not be clearly defined until trained personnel with specialized radiation detection equipment are on the scene. Having onsite radiological detection capability could reduce the negative impact of radiation exposure to event attendees.

NUCLEAR

Nuclear terrorism involves the detonation or threatened detonation of a nuclear bomb or the compromise of an existing nuclear facility, and refers to the use of nuclear materials as weapons.

Although the use of a crude nuclear weapon makes the threat of nuclear terrorism possible, FBI intelligence suggests that it would be difficult for a group to construct such a weapon without weapons-grade uranium or plutonium.

EXPLOSIVES

Explosives are defined as materials that are capable of violent decomposition. This decomposition often takes the form of extremely rapid oxidation (burning). Explosions are the result of a sudden and violent release of gas during the decomposition of explosive substances. High temperature, strong shock, and a loud noise follow this release. Explosives are classified according to the speed of their decomposition.

Because they are readily available, explosives are the most common weapons of mass destruction. When you plan an event, find out:

- Who is the local responder for possible explosives or suspicious packages?
- Does your community have a bomb squad?
- Do you have dogs that are trained to identify explosives?
- What is the community policy on explosive devices?

Explosives seem to be the weapon of choice for terrorists. Less than 5 percent of actual or attempted bombings are preceded by a threat. The lack of prior notification makes casualties more likely than if a notice is given. The explosives can deliver various levels of destruction and can provide a vehicle for the dispersal of chemical, biological, incendiary, and nuclear agents.

The job aids, Bomb Threat Checklist and Bomb Threat Standoff, are included on pages A-85 and A-86, respectively, of Appendix A: Job Aids.

Explosives produce four effects when detonated:

- Blast pressure
- Fragmentation
- Thermal effect
- Ground shock

INCENDIARY DEVICES

As a subset of explosives, incendiary devices have been used by terrorists for many years, because they are flexible tools capable of causing property damage, loss of life, and panic. Incendiary devices continue to spread until fuel is gone or the device is extinguished.

Incendiary devices can be classified as:

- Chemical reaction (including burning fuse)
- Electronic ignition
- Mechanical ignition

The type and construction is limited only to the creativity of the builder.

Incendiary devices may be stationary (placed), hand-thrown (Molotov cocktail), or self-propelled, such as rockets or rifle grenades.

INCENDIARY DEVICES (CONTINUED)

The components of an incendiary device are the ignition source, combustible filler material, and housing or container.

DETECTION

To detect an incendiary device, combustible gas meters, flame ionization detectors, trained dogs, photoionization detectors, and colorimetric tubes may be used.

The clues are similar to detection clues for arson. The clues should be a signal for the responder to take appropriate actions to safeguard him- or herself and the public and treat the area as a potential crime scene. The signs include:

- Prior warning (phone calls)
- Multiple fire locations
- Signs of accelerants
- Containers from flammable liquids
- Splatter patterns indicating a thrown device
- Fusing residue
- Signs of forced entry to the area
- Common appliances out of place for the environment

Incendiary devices may be made with:

- Roadway flares
- Gasoline and motor oil
- Light bulbs
- Common electrical components and devices
- Matches and other household chemicals
- Fireworks
- Propane and butane cylinders
- Plastic pipes, bottles, and cans

MITIGATING ACTIONS

Unattended Packages

At every event, people will leave some items unattended. Public safety officials must decide beforehand how to handle these items. Who will respond? Does the community have dogs trained to identify explosives? Will the area be evacuated? Decide these issues ahead of time and have a written plan for all public safety personnel to follow.

Concealment Areas

Concealment areas are areas where persons may hide or conceal packages or other weapons. The best way to avoid problems in these areas is to map the event grounds and identify the areas that could be used as hiding places. The venue staff could assist police in this matter.

Security Sweeps

How often is security going to go through the event site? What are they looking for? How do they handle incidents? Who is going to do the sweep? Venue personnel and security personnel should work together. These are a few areas to address in advance. After a sweep of the area has been completed, the area must be secured.

SUICIDE BOMBERS

Another terrorist tactic currently used frequently in foreign countries involves suicide bombers who carry the explosives concealed on their persons, and detonate them in crowded areas such as restaurants, nightclubs, public transit buses, or areas of mass gatherings.

Because suicide bombers are unconcerned with capture, they are difficult to plan for and to respond to. Emergency response planning should carefully consider how to deal with this type of threat at a special event. Additionally, planners cannot discount the potential for terrorists to employ multiple suicide bombers in which the first attack is designed to cause casualties and draw emergency responders to the scene specifically to expose them to a second suicide bomber attack.

RESPONSE PROCEDURES

Local WMD/CBRNE response protocols should be in place in public safety emergency response agencies at this time. As part of the planning process, these procedures should be reviewed, and created or modified as necessary. If a WMD/CBRNE incident occurs during the special event, local response agency protocols should be followed.

ELECTRICAL UTILITY COORDINATION REQUIREMENTS

Participants, spectators, and event staff are all affected by lighting, which is needed to set up, tear down, and ensure the safety of the event. Make certain that lighting is adequate and that the power supply to provide the lighting for the event, campgrounds, and parking areas is adequate.

Even in venues that are darkened for performances, lighting should always be in use to identify exits as well as the corridors and aisles leading to them. All temporary electrical facilities should be inspected and approved by a local government inspector to ensure the safety of all.

Install auxiliary battery power or generators to provide light and to power the public-address system during power outage. You must be able to give information and directions to spectators during a power failure to alleviate panic.

Because many concerts are performed with only stage lighting, event staff access to the main lighting board or house lights console is essential in case of an emergency. Onsite personnel responsible for dealing with emergencies must know the location of the controls for these lights and how to operate them.

A Utilities Department Venue Assessment Checklist is included on pages A-40 and A-41 of Appendix A: Job Aids.

FIRE SAFETY

All States and territories have legislation governing fire safety. The local fire authority should monitor fire prevention and preparedness plans to ensure that the measures taken meet relevant standards and comply with State/local life safety codes. Fire safety officials should conduct an onsite inspection in advance of the event, and ensure that any deficiencies noted are corrected prior to the event.

Organizers and health personnel should consider potential fire hazards in the planning process and discuss with the fire authority any concerns they may have. Concerns should include designating smoking areas and providing proper cigarette disposal receptacles.

Fire and law enforcement agencies should determine in advance how they will handle a civil disturbance or riot involving fire-setting behavior and have contingency plans in place. For example, a team of police officers may be assigned to accompany each engine sent out to quell a fire set by rioters.

Site design should be such as to mitigate fire hazards. For example, clear storage areas, timeliness in picking up trash, construction of metal rather than wood, no open flames, and control of pyrotechnics, assist in fire mitigation.

FIRE SAFETY (CONTINUED)

When the event includes fireworks, fire service personnel should conduct a diligent search for any unexploded fireworks. Before you allow public access to the area, safely collect and remove any unexploded fireworks.

A Fire Services Venue Assessment Checklist is included on pages A-49 and A-50 of Appendix A: Job Aids.

COMMUNICATIONS SYSTEMS

A means of communicating with the crowd is essential at all events. Ideally, you should establish multiple communications systems to enable messages to be directed at different sections of the crowd, including crowds massed outside the venue. The Incident Command Post should have access to the central communications system, and interoperability and communications with the jurisdiction's Emergency Operations Center (EOC) if it is activated during the event.

Before the event begins, establish appropriate arrangements for communications if an emergency arises. If emergency personnel will use a separate sound system, they need some means of muting or silencing the stage sound system. Also, consider the use of signboards throughout the venue as an enhancement to the public-address system.

Because public announcements are an important element of the safety plan for an event, consider the style and content of announcements, as follows:

- At what volume level can announcements be heard over spectator noise?
- Will the audience easily understand announcements?
- Are multiple-language announcements required?
- What wording will lend credibility to the instructions?

If public-address systems cannot be put in place outside the venue, personnel can use the public-address systems that form part of the electronic siren system in most emergency vehicles.

Closed-circuit television is another option available for organizers to provide visual information to the public.

INTEROPERABLE COMMUNICATIONS

While it goes without saying that the various emergency services (police, health, fire) must be able to communicate with their own staffs, experience has shown that different services must be able to:

- Communicate with each other.
- Communicate between staff outside and inside the venue to obtain a proper understanding of the nature or scope of an emergency.
- Communicate with senior event organizers, including security personnel, who may be the first to identify an incipient problem.

INTEROPERABLE COMMUNICATIONS (CONTINUED)

Consider the following suggestions:

- Do not rely on cellular telephones.
- Ensure there is an integrated, multi-agency frequency for communications.
- Consider laying land lines for telephone service.
- Include the use of amateur radio operators for communications.

A central communications area (for example, a room or a trailer dedicated to this use) at the Incident Command Post with a representative from each major agency may facilitate the dissemination of vital information through the centralized monitoring of relevant radio communications.

Because a single system can fail, the communications system should be multi-modal. It should also be supplied with its own backup power source.

ATTENDEES' PERSONAL EMERGENCIES

Some means should be established to contact spectators and for spectators to call outside the venue if necessary. Some events provide small booths staffed with volunteers to assist in message passing. Other events use the public address system. Still others provide event brochures with emergency information inside. Select the most effective way to send messages at your event. If invited to, many phone companies often will provide a temporary bank of pay or credit card phones at the venue.

EVENT PUBLIC ADDRESS SYSTEM

Do not rely on the sound system used by the performers to serve internal requirements and release information to the public. Sometimes those responsible for performers' sound systems have refused to authorize their use except during a change of performers. So, an alternate venue-wide PA system is necessary to prevent delays in relaying messages. Informing the public of information reduces the pressures on event staff. Reducing uncertainty among spectators defuses tension. A public-address system is important at any event.

EVENT EMERGENCY WARNING SYSTEM

Some means to inform everyone of an emergency or dangerous weather condition should be in place for every event, no matter the size. This emergency warning system must be able to operate without benefit of the main power source and must be operational at all times. Ensure that the system can be heard clearly in all areas of the event. One person should be in charge of emergency communications. The Incident Commander should authorize the release of emergency messages. All involved agencies should be advised, in advance if possible, of the anticipated release of an emergency message and allowed to inform their personnel to prepare for the public's response. Part of the planning process should be drafting sample pre-scripted messages for use in an emergency. While drafting these messages, consider using a code word or phrase to identify authentic emergency messages and to ensure that emergency personnel respond only to true emergencies.

RUMOR CONTROL

Rumor Control is another area that is difficult to plan for but one that you must address. Most communities have plans for rumor control during emergencies. You can respond in a similar manner to rumors during an incident at an event. As discussed in Chapter 3, the lead agency should designate a Public Information Officer (PIO). Upon designation, the lead agency must determine in advance both what is going to be said and who is authorized to release information. For accuracy and to promote efficiency in rumor control, designate one source of authority.

Internal rumor control is also needed. Personnel working the event need to be kept informed through an official chain of communication, especially if an unanticipated incident occurs. Information is best disseminated through daily shift briefings that include the sharing of operational objectives for the Operational Period.

OCCUPATIONAL HEALTH AND SAFETY

Because the promoter and authorities are obligated to provide for the safety of the audience, as well as appropriate care, safety, and training of all personnel working at the event, they should be familiar with State and local occupational health and safety legislation.

Many events rely on staff volunteers. While most public safety agencies are not permitted to use volunteers because the agencies may be liable for them, the promoter will probably use volunteers extensively and is liable for their safety. Emergency Medical Services (EMS) may use volunteers, provided that they are adequately trained and certified. If the public-sector agencies use volunteers, they must protect the volunteers as they would protect the occupational health and safety of any other employee.

At events where noise levels are high, such as rock concerts, air shows, and motor racing events, adequate hearing protection must be provided to employees who will be exposed to high noise levels for prolonged periods.

Noise pollution from events probably causes the majority of complaints to authorities from the surrounding community, and some means of monitoring and reducing noise levels should be implemented, if possible. The permitting agency should mandate that the promoter advise the community of what to expect well in advance of the event.

ALCOHOL, DRUGS, AND WEAPONS

Alcohol, drugs, and weapons are potential hazards that members of the crowd might bring to any event. They can be catalysts for, and can exacerbate, unruly behavior in a crowd. Every community has its own laws and regulations regarding alcohol, drugs, and weapons. The following suggestions are merely guidelines.

A number of strategies that have been implemented, with varying degrees of success, in reducing the problem include:

- Consider the prohibition of the sale and use of alcoholic beverages at events where unruly audiences are expected, or where a significant number of the patrons will be under the legal drinking age.
- If alcohol is to be sold, then low-alcohol-content beverages can be made available. Alcohol sale times can be controlled and beverages dispensed only in disposable cups.
- Establish an early "last call" for alcohol. For example, during major-league baseball games, alcohol is not sold after the seventh inning, and during professional basketball games, it is not sold after the third quarter.
- If alcohol, weapons, and fireworks are lawful within the State, advance tickets and display advertising should contain the message that they will not be permitted into the event. Tickets and advertising should also state that the purchase of tickets is deemed to constitute the patron's consent to be searched for prohibited material prior to admission.
- Searches of personal belongings (such as jackets, purses, or bags) and confiscation of any alcohol, drugs-and weapons further reduces the risk of unruly behavior.
- Signs in event parking areas and at admission gates should also display a warning to discourage patrons from bringing alcohol, drugs, or weapons into the event. There are, however, possible negative consequences to such signage. Some patrons may attempt to consume a quantity of alcohol intended for the entire event prior to entry, ultimately causing problems for the event medical staff. Alternatively, signage could also have the effect of causing spectators to leave alcohol in their cars, only to consume it in the parking lot at the end of the event prior to departure. The most desirable action is to discourage patrons from bringing prohibited materials to the event in the first place.

Three strategies that may be applied to handling all prohibited material include:

- Give the spectator the option of returning the material to his or her car, with a subsequent loss of place in line.
- If you decide to confiscate prohibited goods, you must make arrangements for the storage and disposal of these materials.
- Tag it with peel-and-stick numbered stickers for return to the patron following the event. If, for any reason, you deem confiscation inappropriate, you can apply such a solution to any weapons, or materials that are potential weapons.

SECURITY

Event organizers must decide what type of security to provide and the scope of the security services' jurisdiction. Providing security services and the stewarding function are vital to public safety, particularly within the venue. There are essentially three types of security that you can provide at large public events. These are:

- Peer security
- Private uniformed security guards
- Uniformed police officers

PEER SECURITY

Experience has shown that, in general, you can promote security for events that attract youth audiences better and more simply through the use of "peer security"—security personnel of the approximate age of the spectators who can relate to and be accepted by the youthful patron. Peer security personnel usually wear brightly colored T-shirts plainly marked SECURITY. They provide a less confrontational security presence by avoiding the posture of rigid authority and the force that often accompanies it. As one concert organizer commented on his experience with peer security:

> "They do not carry weapons and do not attempt to fill a police function. They serve as crowd monitors, people movers, and troubleshooters. Such personnel are not there to reform or catch the alcohol or drug user. . . . They concentrate on maintaining orderly crowd flow for the safety of the patrons."

> "You should provide appropriate guidelines for peer security personnel and stipulate limits to their authority, such as: keeping the peace, helping people in distress, assisting the staff of doctors and nurses, clearing paths for ambulances, seeing that areas were cleared for helicopter take-offs and landings, and guarding the stage, and the performers."

PRIVATE UNIFORMED SECURITY GUARDS

Private uniformed security guards are probably better suited to events that attract more docile spectators, such as religious rallies, charitable dinners, and art shows, and they usually will be less costly than a police presence. At events attracting crowds of more youthful exuberance, or volatile sports spectators, private uniformed security guards are probably more appropriately utilized in non-confrontational roles, such as taking tickets and parking cars.

Care needs to be taken to ensure that private uniformed security personnel are recruited only from reputable sources with competent and suitably trained personnel. You should discuss any special requirements for the event with the security firm.

In certain circumstances, the use of private uniformed security guards can lead to problems. A uniform gives an authoritative appearance that is often not supported either by adequate training or authority in law. As a result, private uniformed security personnel provide neither the power of police nor the rapport achieved by peer security.

UNIFORMED POLICE OFFICERS

At many events, uniformed police officers perform functions such as traffic control, and leave internal event security to private personnel employed by the organizers.

A typical crowd composed mainly of families needs one police officer per 1,000 spectators. In a more active crowd (for example, at a sporting event where alcoholic beverages are sold), two police officers are commonly employed for every 1,000 spectators.

Certain spectator groups may not, however, be amenable to either peer or private uniformed security, such as crowds who historically have experienced violence as part of the event "culture." While various diffusing techniques are available and should be employed, often nothing less than a contingent of uniformed police will dissuade a spectator group that enters with the expectation and intent of violence. These groups are in marked contrast to rock concert audiences who enter in a peaceful frame of mind, but may be induced to rowdiness by alcohol, shortcomings in the event, or other catalysts.

The composition of security services will vary according to the event; one or a combination of the three types may better serve different events.

SECURITY ROLES AND RESPONSIBILITIES

Clearly establish the roles and responsibilities of security personnel prior to the event. Decisions and actions taken by security personnel may affect the way emergency services and health personnel respond to a crisis. In planning, and throughout all stages of the event, maintain a close working relationship among:

- Security personnel
- The promoter
- Health and medical services
- Other police and emergency services
- Other security services (for example, those who are responsible for the performers' personal safety

Special security considerations include:

- Will the event organizers or promoters use police officers for onsite security, or will they hire private security officers?
- If you use private security officers, what will their role and functions be, and how will their services be integrated with those of the police? Are they permitted to work outside of the venue?
- What policies will security personnel enforce for minor offenses onsite to assure that established policy is enforced consistently during the event and throughout the venue?
- Will there be areas onsite for the collection and storage of significant sums of money, and what security will be established to protect these areas, as well as offsite transfer or banking? Are these areas positioned near road access to avoid the risks associated with carrying large sums of money on foot through spectator areas?
- How will security personnel move high-profile persons through crowded areas?

SECURITY ROLES AND RESPONSIBILITIES (CONTINUED)

- How will security personnel handle lost or stolen property?
- How will security personnel detect forged credentials?
- How will security personnel deal with lost children and missing persons?
- Ensure that equal patron assessment and treatment occurs at entrances and security checkpoints. All attendees must be treated as "equal risks" from a security standpoint.

You should clearly define the responsibilities and roles of security personnel before the event. These may include:

- Crowd management, including measures taken to prevent crushing.
- Control of access to stage or performance areas.
- Security control at entrances and exits.
- Area patrol to minimize the risk of fire.
- Control of vehicle traffic and marshaling.
- Searches for alcohol, drugs, and weapons.
- Security of large sums of money and confiscated goods.
- Assistance to emergency services, if necessary.

PRE-EVENT BRIEFING OF SECURITY PERSONNEL

To enable security personnel to perform their duties effectively, you must brief them appropriately prior to the event. This briefing should provide security personnel with:

- Details of the venue footprint and grid map, including entrances, exits, medical aid posts, and any potential hazards.
- Clear direction on the management of unacceptable behavior.
- Basic information about the event, such as the locations of medical aid posts and lost-person stations, information, parking, transportation matters, and other pertinent spectator information.
- Details of emergency and evacuation plans, such as procedures for raising alarms, protocols for requesting assistance, and evacuation procedures.
- Instructions for the operation, deactivation, and isolation of any onsite machinery and utility supply in case of emergency.
- Details of the incident communications plan and the equipment to be used.

The attitude of security personnel has a major influence on crowd compliance. Security personnel are charged with not only controlling a crowd, but also with making them feel welcome. Every individual staff member who comes into contact with the spectators plays a role in crowd control. The dress, demeanor, and actions of staff may set behavioral expectation levels, and you should consider this fact in planning and pre-event briefing of staff.

DEPLOYMENT

You should consider strategic deployment of security staff. All venues will have areas that are particularly suited to crowd monitoring and problem areas where particular attention is required. The type and size of the venue may control what method of transportation the security personnel use. Using bicycles or golf carts may be more practical than deploying in vehicles or on foot. Indoor events are usually patrolled on foot, while a large outdoor area may be patrolled using bicycles, golf carts, or automobiles. The amount of time during which the personnel must patrol also may be a factor. Deployment considerations include:

- Identification of strategic deployment points, such as entrances and exits, barriers, and general thoroughfares.
- Establishment of strategic observation points to monitor crowd movements and behavior (A central control room with video surveillance may be required.)
- Use of video pole cameras in densely populated areas.

DIGNITARIES AND CELEBRITY GUESTS

Events with invited dignitaries or in which dignitaries participate create an entirely new group of hazards and difficulties. A dignitary presence may change the level of jurisdiction and the type of security needed at the event. The planning team may not know in advance if a dignitary or celebrity is coming. Therefore, it is important to have contingency plans involving local agencies such as law enforcement, fire, and others to coordinate with the State and Federal agencies if a special guest arrives. Many dignitaries have their own security service that travels with them. Providing special seating for dignitaries may be necessary. Discuss the possible difficulties and hazards before allowing the promoter or sponsor to extend invitations to dignitaries.

A Law Enforcement Venue Assessment Checklist is included on pages A-51 and A-52 of Appendix A: Job Aids.

LOST-CHILD AND "MEET ME" LOCATIONS

Because of the size of an event and the number of spectators at the venue, children will inevitably be separated from their adult supervisors. Planners must designate a place for lost children to be reunited with their parents or guardians and have a checklist to allow information to be disseminated quickly and accurately. Issues regarding legal custody of minor children may be a consideration, and would probably be best dealt with by law enforcement agencies onsite.

Other useful areas include "meet me" locations. These are designated locations throughout the site, which are well marked and easily spotted. Patrons can plan to meet at these locations at a predetermined time, or they may use these locations if they become separated.

INFORMATION CENTER

A well-identified, well-publicized information center onsite, staffed with knowledgeable personnel, can reduce pressures on security, medical, and other event staff, by providing a full range of informational services to patrons. Reduction of uncertainty among spectators defuses the kind of tension that can lead to behavioural problems. To ease the burden on the public sector, the promoter should be required in the permit application process to provide this service.

PLAN FOR "MURPHY'S LAW"

As the title for this section suggests, organizers cannot plan for or anticipate every crisis. You can, however, take certain measures to ensure personnel safety. For example, if a stand collapses, the fire department routinely uses an established, practiced procedure to remove the injured and to cordon off the area. This procedure will not change simply because the stand collapses at a spontaneous event. Contingency plans, modeled on established procedures, need to be in place for demonstrations, protests, or picketing that may occur during a planned event. Train for the worst and respond to your training. Plan for the worst, and you can handle even the unexpected events in an orderly manner. Designate specific incident resources in advance to respond to spontaneous events as they may occur. During event planning, brainstorm a list of the potential spontaneous events that are most likely to occur.

CHAPTER 3: INCIDENT COMMAND AND CONTROL

INTRODUCTION

Chapter One stresses the importance of pre-event planning, organization, and leadership. It suggests a planning team using the Incident Command System (ICS) to manage the event planning process effectively. In a large-scale event involving numerous agencies, people can become confused as to who is in charge, what role everyone plays, and what responsibilities everyone has. ICS is an excellent tool that can resolve these issues. This chapter discusses ICS, how it can be applied to special events, and the concept of Unified Command.

Unfortunately, even the best-planned special events may not run entirely smoothly. During any special event, you must be prepared to respond to one or more incidents that may occur during the event. The way these incidents are managed has a great deal to do with the ultimate success of the special event. Everyone must know his or her role and tasks, and where to seek information. This chapter also discusses the use of ICS during these situations.

INCIDENT COMMAND SYSTEM (ICS)

The Incident Command System (ICS) dates back to the early 1970s. Responding to a series of wildland fires in Southern California, municipal, State, county, and Federal resources worked together to achieve a single goal. Because agency differences in communications, control, strategy management, and other leadership concerns, as well as the use of nonstandard terminology, caused many difficulties, the agencies produced a plan called FIRESCOPE to combat these problems and create centralized control. The National Fire Academy adopted this program, and the International Association of Chiefs of Police endorsed it in 1987.

The Federal Government endorsed this plan and now requires its use as outlined in Homeland Security Presidential Directive – 5 (HSPD-5) in any operation in the form of the National Incident Management System (NIMS).

The NIMS represents a core set of doctrine, concepts, principles, terminology, and organizational processes to enable effective, efficient, and collaborative incident management at all levels. It is not an operational incident management or resource allocation plan. To this end, HSPD-5 requires the Secretary of Homeland Security to develop a National Response Plan (NRP) that integrates Federal Government domestic prevention, preparedness, response, and recovery plans into a single, all-disciplines, all-hazards plan. The NRP, using the comprehensive framework provided by the NIMS, will provide the structure and mechanisms for national-level policy and operational direction for Federal support to State, local, and tribal incident managers and for exercising direct Federal authorities and responsibilities as appropriate under the law.

INCIDENT COMMAND SYSTEM (ICS) (CONTINUED)

Using ICS is an excellent means of determining how resources are going to be used, who will coordinate them, and how information will be communicated, using common terminology in response to a variety of matters relating to any special event. ICS is designed to assist event planners in the areas of:

- Basic management of resources
- Organization
- Delegation of authority
- Coordination
- Communication
- Evaluation

The use of ICS optimizes communication and coordination, and facilitates the protection of life and property. ICS achieves this goal by establishing a protocol command structure for any event or incident. Using common terminology ensures that everyone will understand what is being said and how to acknowledge it properly. The command organization consists of an Incident Commander, Command Staff, and General Staff. In some small events, the Incident Commander (IC) may handle all functions; in larger events, the IC may delegate tasks to other persons. Five functional components of ICS are implemented, as needed:

- Command
- Planning Section
- Operations Section
- Logistics Section
- Finance/Administration Section

In addition to the type, location, size, and expected duration of the event, the following information will help event planners develop an organizational structure to meet the management needs of the planned event:

- Does the event involve a single agency or multiple agencies?
- Does the event involve a single jurisdiction or multiple jurisdictions?
- What Command Staff needs exist?
- What kind, type and amounts of resources are required by the event?
- Are there any projected aviation operations?
- Are there any staging areas and other required facilities?
- What kind and type of logistical support needs are required by the event?
- Are there any known limitations or restrictions of local resources?
- What kind and type of communications resources are available?

ICS can be expanded as the event demands increase in volume or complexity, and then contracted as demands diminish.

INCIDENT COMMAND SYSTEM (ICS) (CONTINUED)

Applying ICS to special events is logical and relatively straightforward. As discussed in Chapter One, the representative from the special event's lead agency is a likely candidate for Incident Commander. The Incident Commander or planning team leader could divide the event into Operational Periods (e.g., the day before, day of, or first 12-hours, second 12-hours, etc.). An Incident Action Plan (IAP) is then developed for each Operational Period. The IAP identifies the objectives and actions of all involved agencies for that particular Operational Period. Planners can precisely establish what is required before and during the event. An Incident Action Plan schedule and applicable ICS forms are included on pages A-62 through A-80 of Appendix A: Job Aids.

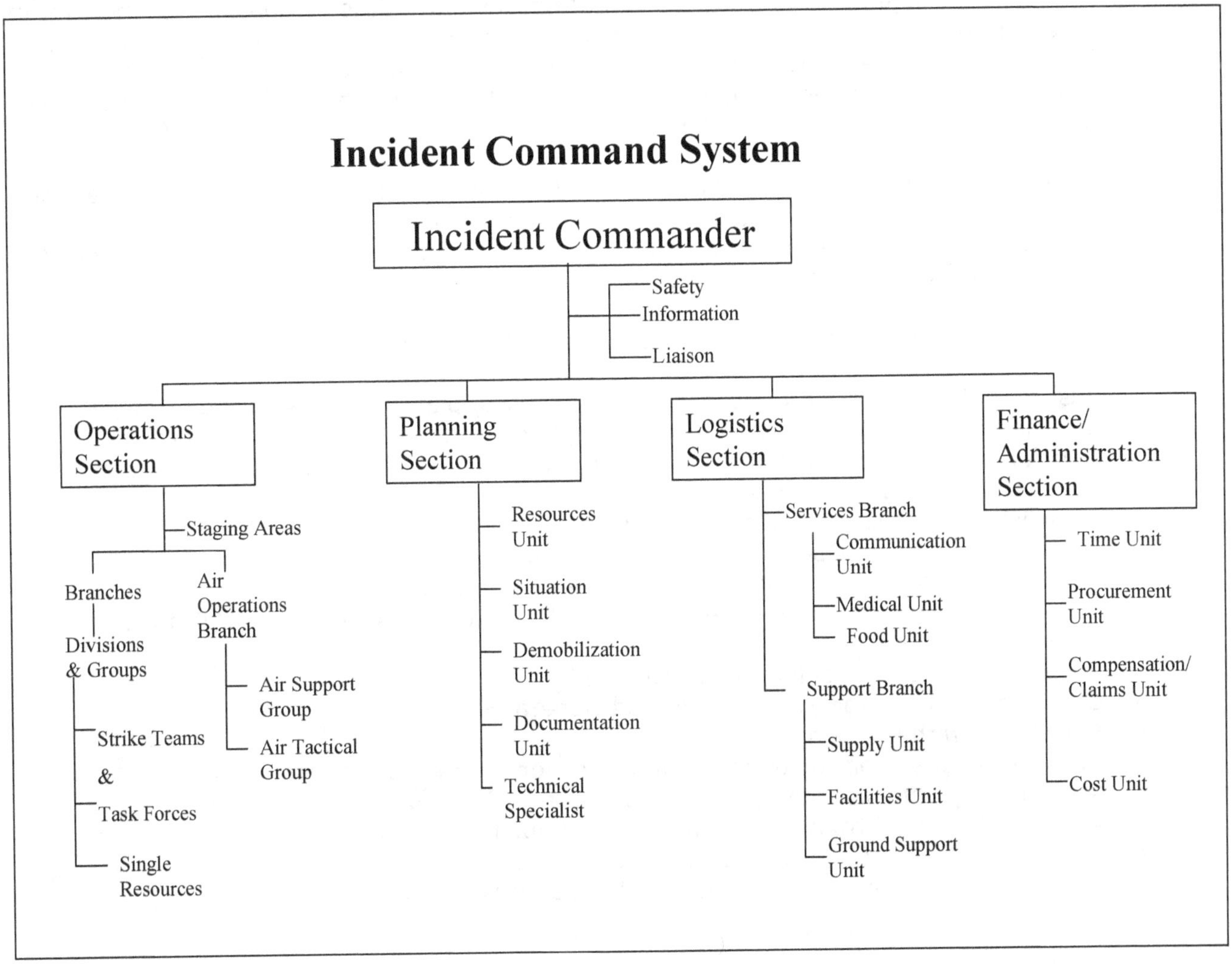

Incident Command System

Incident Commander
- Safety
- Information
- Liaison

Operations Section
- Staging Areas
- Branches
  - Divisions & Groups
    - Strike Teams & Task Forces
    - Single Resources
- Air Operations Branch
  - Air Support Group
  - Air Tactical Group

Planning Section
- Resources Unit
- Situation Unit
- Demobilization Unit
- Documentation Unit
- Technical Specialist

Logistics Section
- Services Branch
  - Communication Unit
  - Medical Unit
  - Food Unit
- Support Branch
  - Supply Unit
  - Facilities Unit
  - Ground Support Unit

Finance/ Administration Section
- Time Unit
- Procurement Unit
- Compensation/ Claims Unit
- Cost Unit

ROLES AND EXPECTATIONS

The ICS chart above shows the five major sections that may be required to manage any event and/or incident. Branches of these sections that may also be needed are identified as well. Some events/incidents require very few functional areas, while others require activation of more. As you can see from the chart, ICS designates positions for every contingency. The job descriptions below detail what is required of persons filling the major positions.

INCIDENT COMMANDER

As discussed in Chapter 1, the event Incident Commander (IC) is responsible for the overall management of the special event. For most events, a single IC carries out the command activity. Certain incidents occurring during a special event may dictate the need for a specific Incident Commander to manage that incident. This IC should report to the overall event IC.

The overall event IC may have a deputy from his or her agency or from an assisting agency. Deputies may also be used at Section and Branch levels of the ICS organization. Deputies must have the same qualifications as the persons for whom they work because they must be ready to take over those positions at any time.

Responsibilities—The overall event Incident Commander must:

- Ensure that all appropriate pre-event risk analyses, plans, checklists, and forms, as provided in Appendix A: Job Aids, are completed and available to event personnel.
- Develop the mission, objectives, strategies, and command structure for the event.
- Establish immediate priorities.
- Establish an appropriately located event Incident Command Post (ICP).
- Develop an effective Operational Period schedule.
- Ensure that planning meetings are scheduled as required.
- Approve and authorize the implementation of an Incident Action Plan (IAP) for each Operational Period.
- Ensure that adequate safety measures are in place.
- Coordinate activity for all Command and General Staff.
- Coordinate with key people.
- Approve requests for additional resources or for the release of resources.
- Keep agency administrators informed of event/incident status.
- Approve the use of trainees, volunteers, and auxiliary personnel.
- Authorize release of information to the news media.
- Approve the demobilization of the event/incident when appropriate.

SAFETY OFFICER

The Safety Officer's function is to develop and recommend measures for assuring personnel safety and assess or anticipate hazardous and unsafe situations. Only one Safety Officer will be assigned for each event. The Safety Officer may have assistants as necessary, and the assistants may also represent assisting agencies or jurisdictions. Safety assistants may have specific responsibilities, such as air operations or hazardous materials.

Responsibilities—The Safety Officer should:

- Participate in all planning meetings.
- Identify hazardous situations associated with the event.
- Review the IAP for safety implications.
- Exercise emergency authority to stop or prevent unsafe acts.
- Investigate accidents that have occurred during the event.
- Assign assistants as needed.
- Review and approve the medical plan.

INFORMATION OFFICER

The Information Officer is responsible for developing and releasing public information regarding safety matters of the event to the news media, to incident personnel, and to other appropriate agencies and organizations. Typically, the event promoter or sponsor releases most public information and advertisements. If a major incident occurs during the event involving those operating under Unified Command, the Information Officer should become the sole spokesperson. The Information Officer may have assistants as necessary, and the assistants may also represent assisting agencies or jurisdictions.

Participating agencies may have conflicting policies and procedures concerning the dissemination of public information. The following major responsibilities assigned to the Information Officer apply generally to any event.

Responsibilities—The Information Officer should:

- Determine from the Incident Commander whether there are any limits on information release.
- Develop material for use in media briefings.
- Obtain the Incident Commander's approval of media releases.
- Establish a media briefing area.
- Inform the media and conduct media briefings.
- Arrange for tours and other interviews or briefings that may be required.
- Obtain media information that may be useful to event planning.
- Maintain current information summaries and/or displays on the event and provide information on the status of any incidents to assigned personnel.

LIAISON OFFICER

Special events that are multi-jurisdictional or that involve several agencies may require the establishment of a Liaison Officer position on the Command Staff.

The Liaison Officer is the contact person for agency representatives from assisting or cooperating agencies who are assigned to the event. These representatives are personnel other than those on direct tactical assignments or those involved in Unified Command.

Responsibilities—The Liaison Officer should:

- Be a contact point for agency representatives.
- Maintain a list of assisting and cooperating agencies and agency representatives.
- Assist in establishing and coordinating interagency contacts.
- Keep agencies supporting the event aware of event/incident status.
- Monitor event operations to identify current or potential inter-organizational problems.
- Participate in planning meetings, providing current resource status, including limitations and capability of assisting agency resources.

OPERATIONS SECTION CHIEF

Responsibilities—The Operations Section Chief should:

- Manage tactical operations.
    - Interact with the next lower level of the Operations Section (Branch, Division/Group) to develop the operations portions of the IAP.
    - Request resources needed to implement the Operation's tactics as a part of the IAP development.
- Assist in developing the operations portion of the IAP.
- Supervise the execution of the IAP for Operations.
    - Maintain close contact with subordinate positions, and
    - Ensure safe tactical operations.
- Request additional resources to support tactical operations.
- Approve release of resources from assigned status (not released from the event/incident).
- Make or approve expedient changes to the IAP during the operational period as necessary.
- Maintain close communication with the IC.

PLANNING SECTION CHIEF

The Planning Section collects, evaluates, processes, and disseminates information for use throughout the event. When activated, the Planning Section Chief who is a member of the General Staff manages the section.

Responsibilities—The Planning Section Chief should:

- Collect and process situation information about the event.
- Establish information requirements and reporting schedules for Planning Section units (Resources and Situation Units).
- Supervise preparation of the IAP.
- Provide input to the Incident Commander and Operations Section Chief in preparing the IAP.
- Establish special information collection activities (for example, weather, environmental, and toxic substances) as necessary.
- Compile and display event status information.
- Report any significant changes in the status of the event.
- Assemble information on alternative strategies.
- Provide periodic predictions on event/incident potential.
- Determine the need for any specialized resources in support of the event.
- Reassign out-of-service personnel already onsite to ICS organizational positions, as appropriate.
- Oversee preparation of event/incident demobilization plan.

LOGISTICS SECTION CHIEF

Typically, the promoter and/or sponsor provide resources to execute the event. However, certain necessary resources and support needs may not be provided (e.g., command post, communications equipment, medical supplies, etc.), and therefore, must be procured. The Logistics Section, with the exception of aviation support, provides support needs for the event command infrastructure. The Air Support Group (in the Air Operations Branch of the Operations Section) handles aviation support. The Logistics Section Chief, who may assign a Deputy, manages the Logistics Section. A Deputy is most often assigned when all designated units within the Logistics Section are activated.

The Logistics Section Chief will determine the need to activate or deactivate a unit. If a unit is not activated, responsibility for that unit's duties will remain with the Logistics Section Chief.

Responsibilities—The Logistics Section Chief should:

- Manage all event command infrastructure logistics.
- Provide logistical input to the Incident Commander in preparing the IAP.
- Brief Branch Directors and Unit Leaders, as needed.
- Identify anticipated and known event service and support requirements.
- Request additional resources, as needed.
- Review and provide input to the Communications Plan, Medical Plan and Traffic Plan.
- Supervise requests for additional resources.
- Oversee demobilization of Logistics Section.

FINANCE/ADMINISTRATION SECTION CHIEF

The Finance/Administration Section is responsible for managing all financial aspects of the event command infrastructure. Here again, typically, the promoter and/or sponsor manage the financial aspects of most special events. When certain necessary resources and support needs are not provided, however, some means of maintaining financial accountability must be established. As such, not all event/incidents will require a Finance/Administration Section. Only when the agencies involved in responding to the event/incident have a specific need for Finance/Administration services will the section be activated.

Responsibilities—The Finance/Administration Section Chief should:

- Manage all financial aspects of an event's command infrastructure.
- Provide financial and cost analysis information, as requested.
- Gather pertinent information from briefings with responsible agencies.
- Develop an operating plan for the Finance/Administration Section to fill supply and support needs.
- Determine the need to set up and operate an event/incident commissary.
- Meet with assisting and cooperating agency representatives as needed.
- Maintain daily contact with agency administrative headquarters on Financial/Administration matters.
- Ensure that all personnel time records are accurately completed and transmitted to home agencies, according to policy.
- Provide financial input to demobilization planning.
- Ensure that all obligation documents initiated at the event/incident are properly prepared and completed.
- Brief agency administrative personnel on all event/incident-related financial matters needing attention or followup.

A sample Expense Report is included on page A-81 of Appendix A: Job Aids.

INCIDENTS OCCURRING DURING A SPECIAL EVENT

As discussed above, certain incidents occurring during a special event may dictate the need for a specific Incident Commander to manage that particular incident (e.g., isolated structure fire, vehicle crash, HazMat incident, structure collapse, multiple casualty incident, etc.). When an incident occurs within a special event, immediate action must be taken to control and manage the incident. As the incident grows, the issues that must be considered will grow as well. The Incident Commander of the special event may assign command of the emergency incident to a ranking responder. This responder must take initial steps to bring order to the incident, just as in situations that require more traditional applications of ICS. The Incident Commander of the special event may authorize the responder to implement his or her own command structure and/or call upon the resources of the event command structure. This responder must:

- Assess the situation.
- Determine whether human life is at immediate risk.
- Establish the immediate priorities and objectives.
- Determine whether there are adequate and appropriate resources on-scene or ordered.
- Establish an appropriately located on-scene Command Post (CP), if needed.
- Establish an appropriate initial command structure, if needed.
- Develop an action plan.
- Ensure that adequate safety measures are in place.
- Coordinate activity for all Command and General Staff.
- Consider whether the span of control is approaching, or will soon approach, practical limits, taking into account the safety of all personnel.
- Determine whether there are any environmental concerns that must be considered.
- Monitor work progress and coordinate with key people.
- Review and modify objectives and adjust the action plan as necessary.
- Approve requests for additional resources or for the release of resources.
- Keep the overall event Incident Commander informed of incident status.
- Authorize release of information to the news media.
- Order the demobilization of the incident, when appropriate.

TRANSFER OF COMMAND

In prolonged events, it is likely that a change of command may take place. When transfer of command is necessary, the transfer must be made as efficiently as possible and in person, whenever possible. To transfer command, the person being relieved must brief the incoming Incident Commander to provide information about:

- The incident conditions:
  - Event history (what has happened so far).
  - The IAP and its current status.
  - Priorities and objectives.
  - Current event organization.
  - Current resource assignments.
  - Resources ordered/needed.
  - Status of communications.
- Safety considerations and concerns.
- Deployment and assignment of operating units and personnel.
- Constraints or limitations on response agencies.
- Incident potential.

  ICS Form 201 is well designed for briefings (ICS Form 201-Incident Briefing form, and instructions for completing the form, are included on pages A-63 through A-68 of Appendix A: Job Aids) because it contains a place for a sketch map, a place to write a summary of current actions and organizational framework, and a place to summarize resources. Sections of the form can be separated from the document and given to ICS sections to complete as needed.

Be aware that changes may cause disruptions, so they should be implemented at the start of Operational Periods, whenever possible. Finally, when command has been transferred, ensure that all personnel and communications centers are notified of the transfer of command.

UNIFIED COMMAND

Unified Command is a term referring to shared responsibility for event management, using either single agency multi-jurisdiction or multiple agencies. A clear line of authority for decisionmaking must always be in place.

ICS offers two options for command, as follows:

- <u>Single Command</u>, in which there is no overlap of jurisdiction or when the agency in charge designates Single Incident Command.

- <u>Unified Command</u>, when more than one agency shares responsibility for responding to, or participating in, the event/incident. Unified Command means that all agencies contribute to the command process by determining goals and objectives, jointly planning activities, conducting integrated tactical operations, and maximizing all resources. Unified Command is also used when an event/incident is multi-jurisdictional or when more than one individual shares overall management responsibility.

Unified Command is a team process, allowing all agencies with responsibility for an incident, either geographical or functional, to establish a common set of incident objectives and strategies to which all can subscribe. This set of objectives and strategies is accomplished without losing or abdicating agency authority, responsibility, or accountability. Unified Command is not a new organization; the U.S. military has used similar command structures in joint operations for years.

There are four elements to consider when applying Unified Command to an event/incident:

POLICIES, OBJECTIVES, STRATEGIES

In ICS, the responsibility to set policies, objectives and strategies belongs to the various jurisdictional and agency administrators who are accountable to their agencies. This activity is accomplished in advance of tactical operations, and it may be coordinated from some location other than the one where the direct action takes place.

ORGANIZATION

In ICS, Unified Command organization consists of the various jurisdictional or agency on-scene senior representatives (agency Incident Commanders).

RESOURCES

In ICS Unified Command, resources are the personnel and equipment supplied by the jurisdictions and agencies that have functional or jurisdictional responsibility for the IAP.

OPERATIONS

In ICS Unified Command, after the objectives, strategies, and interagency agreements are decided, a single party is designated to develop tactical action plans and to direct tactical operations. That person is the Operations Section Chief.

In ICS Unified Command, resources remain under the administrative and policy control of their agencies. However, they respond operationally to mission assignment under the coordination and direction of the Operations Section Chief, depending upon the requirements of the action plan.

Unified Command represents an important element in increasing the effectiveness of multi-jurisdictional or multi-agency events/incidents. As events/incidents become more complex and involve more agencies, the need for Unified Command becomes even greater.

The advantages of using Unified Command include:

- A single set of objectives developed for the entire event/incident.
- A collective approach toward the development of strategies to achieve event/incident goals.
- Improved information flow and coordination among all jurisdictions and agencies involved in the IAP.
- An understanding among agencies of respective priorities and restrictions regarding responsibility for the IAP.
- No compromise or neglect of an agency's authority or legal requirements.
- An awareness among agencies of respective plans, actions, and constraints.
- An optimized combined effort of all agencies performing their respective assignments under a single IAP.
- A reduction or elimination of duplicative efforts, thus reducing cost and chances for frustration and conflict.

Using Unified Command is practical and cost effective. Agencies can improve incident management and achieve goals in a timely, cost-effective manner.

UNIFIED COMMAND ORGANIZATION

Five important features of a Unified Command organization include a single, integrated incident organization; collocated facilities; a single planning process and IAP; shared planning, logistical, and finance sections; and unified resource ordering.

A SINGLE INTEGRATED INCIDENT ORGANIZATION

Under Unified Command, the various jurisdictions or agencies are blended together into an integrated, unified team. The resulting organization may be a mix of personnel from several jurisdictions or from a single agency, each performing appropriate functions and working toward a common set of objectives. The proper mix of participants in a Unified Command organization will depend on:

- The location of the event/incident, which often determines the jurisdictions that must be involved.
- The kind of event/incident, which dictates the functional agencies of the involved jurisdiction(s), as well as other associated agencies.

In a multi-jurisdictional response to an event/incident, a Unified Command structure could consist of a single responsible official from each jurisdiction. In other cases, Unified Command may consist of several functional department managers or assigned representatives from within a single political jurisdiction.

MULTI-AGENCY COORDINATION SYSTEMS

DEFINITION

Multi-agency coordination systems are a combination of facilities, equipment, personnel, procedures, and communications integrated into a common system with responsibility for coordinating and supporting domestic incident management activities. The primary functions of multi-agency coordination systems are to:

- Support incident management policies and priorities.
- Facilitate logistics support and resource tracking.
- Inform resource allocation decisions based on incident management priorities.
- Coordinate incident related information.
- Coordinate interagency and intergovernmental issues regarding incident management policies, priorities, and strategies.

Direct tactical and operational responsibility for the conduct of incident management activities rests with the Incident Commander.

SYSTEM ELEMENTS

Multi-agency coordination systems may contain EOCs and (in certain multi-jurisdictional or complex incident-management situations) multi-agency coordinating entities.

EMERGENCY OPERATIONS CENTER

For purposes of this document, EOCs represent the physical location where the coordination of information and resources to support incident management activities normally takes place. The Incident Command Post (ICP), located at or in the immediate vicinity of an incident site, although primarily focused on the tactical on-scene response, may perform an EOC-like function in smaller-scale incidents, or during the initial phase of the response to larger, more complex events. Standing EOCs, or those activated to support larger, more complex events are typically established in a more central or permanently established facility, at a higher level of organization within a jurisdiction. Department Operations Centers (DOCs) are those facilities organized by major functional discipline (fire, law enforcement, medical services, etc.), or by jurisdiction (city, county, region, etc.), or, more likely, some combination thereof. DOCs normally focus on internal agency incident management and response and are linked to, and, in most cases, are physically represented in a higher level EOC. ICPs should also be linked to DOCs and EOCs to ensure effective and efficient incident management.

For complex incidents, EOCs may be staffed by personnel representing multiple jurisdictions and functional disciplines and a wide variety of resources. For example, a local EOC established in response to a bioterrorism incident would likely include a mix of law enforcement, emergency management, public health, and medical personnel, including representatives of health care facilities, pre-hospital emergency medical services (EMS/EMT), patient transportation systems, pharmaceutical repositories, laboratories, etc. EOCs may be permanent organizations and facilities or may be established to meet temporary, short-term needs. The physical size, staffing, and equipping of an EOC will depend on the size of the jurisdiction, resources available, and anticipated incident-management workload. EOCs may be organized and staffed in a variety of ways. Regardless of the specific organizational structure used, EOCs should include the following core functions:

- Coordination.
- Communications.
- Resource dispatch and tracking.
- Information collection, analysis, and dissemination.

EOCs may also support multi-agency coordination and joint information activities as discussed below.

Upon activation of a local EOC, communications and coordination must be established between the IC/UC and the EOC, when they are not collocated. ICS field organizations must also establish communications with the activated local EOC, either directly or through their parent organizations. Additionally, EOCs at all levels of government and across functional agencies must be capable of communicating appropriately with other EOCs during incidents, to include those maintained by private organizations. Communications between EOCs must be reliable and contain built-in redundancies. The efficient functioning of EOCs most frequently depends on the existence of mutual aid agreements and joint communications protocols among participating agencies.

MULTI-AGENCY COORDINATION ENTITIES

In the case of incidents that cross disciplinary or jurisdictional boundaries or those that involve complex incident-management scenarios, a multi-agency coordination entity, such as an emergency management agency, may be used to facilitate incident management and policy coordination. The situation at hand and the needs of the jurisdictions involved will dictate how these multi-agency coordination entities conduct their business, as well as how they are structured. Multi-agency coordination entities typically consist of principals (or their designees) from organizations and agencies with direct incident management responsibility or with significant incident management support or resource responsibilities. These entities are sometimes referred to as crisis action teams, policy committees, incident management groups, executive teams, or other similar terms.[6] In some instances, EOCs may serve a dual function as a multi-agency coordination entity; in others, the preparedness organizations may fulfill this role. Regardless of the term or organizational structure used, these entities typically provide strategic coordination during domestic incidents. If constituted separately, multi-agency coordination entities, preparedness organizations, and EOCs must coordinate and communicate with one another to provide uniform and consistent guidance to incident management personnel.

Regardless of form or structure, the principal functions and responsibilities of multi-agency coordination entities typically include the following:

1. Ensuring that each agency involved in incident management activities is providing appropriate situational awareness and resource status information.
2. Establishing priorities between incidents and/or Area Commands in concert with the IC/UC(s) involved.
3. Acquiring and allocating resources required by incident management personnel in concert with the priorities established by the IC/UC.
4. Anticipating and identifying future resource requirements.
5. Coordinating and resolving policy issues arising from the incident(s).
6. Providing strategic coordination as required.

Following incidents, multi-agency coordination entities are also typically responsible for ensuring that improvements in plans, procedures, communications, staffing, and other capabilities necessary for improved incident management are acted upon. These improvements should also be coordinated with appropriate preparedness organizations, if these organizations are constituted separately.

---

[6] For example, the wildland fire community has such an entity called the Multi-Agency Coordination Group (MAC Group).

PUBLIC INFORMATION SYSTEMS

Systems and protocols for communicating timely and accurate information to the public are critical during crisis or emergency situations. This section describes the principles, system components, and procedures needed to support effective emergency public information operations.

PUBLIC INFORMATION PRINCIPLES

The PIO supports the Incident Command. Under ICS, the Public Information Officer (PIO) is a key staff member supporting the incident command structure. The PIO represents and advises the Incident Command on all public information matters relating to the management of the incident. The PIO handles:

- Media and public inquiries.
- Emergency public information and warnings.
- Rumor monitoring and response.
- Media monitoring.
- Other functions required to coordinate, clear with appropriate authorities, and disseminate accurate and timely information related to the incident, particularly regarding information on public health and safety and protection.

The PIO is also responsible for coordinating public information at or near the incident site and serving as the on-scene link to the Joint Information System (JIS). In a large-scale operation, the on-scene PIO serves as a field PIO with links to the Joint Information Center (JIC) typically collocated with the Federal, regional, State, local, or tribal EOC tasked with primary incident coordination responsibilities. The JIS provides the mechanism for integrating public information activities among JICs, across jurisdictions, and with the private sector and non-governmental organizations.

Public information functions must be coordinated and integrated across jurisdictions and across functional agencies; among Federal, State, local, and tribal partners; and with the private sector and non-governmental organizations. During emergencies, the public may receive information from a variety of sources. The JIC provides a location for organizations participating in the management of an incident to work together to ensure that timely, accurate, easy-to-understand, and consistent information is disseminated to the public. The JIC is composed of representatives from each organization involved in the management of an incident. In large or complex incidents, particularly those involving complex medical and public health information requirements, JICs may be established at various levels of government. All JICs must communicate and coordinate with each other on an ongoing basis. Public awareness functions must also be coordinated with the information- and operational-security matters that are the responsibility of the information and intelligence function of the ICS, particularly where public awareness activities may affect information or operations security.

Organizations participating in incident management retain independence. ICs and multi-agency coordination entities are responsible for establishing and overseeing JICs to include processes for coordinating and clearing public communications. In the case of UC, the departments, agencies, organizations, or jurisdictions that contribute to joint public information management do not lose their individual identities or responsibility for their own programs or policies. Rather, each entity contributes to the overall unified message.

System Description and Components

Joint Information System

The JIS provides an organized, integrated, and coordinated mechanism to ensure the delivery of understandable, timely, accurate, and consistent information to the public in a crisis. It includes the plans, protocols, and structures that are used to provide information to the public during incident operations, and it encompasses all public information operations related to an incident, including all Federal, State, local, tribal and private organization PIOs, staff, and JICs established to support an incident.

Key elements of the JIS include:

1. Interagency coordination and integration.
2. Developing and delivering coordinated messages.
3. Support for decisionmakers.
4. Flexibility, modularity, and adaptability.

Joint Information Center

A JIC is a physical location where public affairs professionals from organizations involved in incident management activities can collocate to perform critical emergency information, crisis communications, and public-affairs functions. It is important at all times for the JIC to have the most current and accurate information regarding incident management activities. The JIC provides the organizational structure for coordinating and disseminating official information. JICs may be established at each level of incident management as required.

Key points about the JIS include:

1. The JIC must include representatives of each jurisdiction, agency, private sector, and non-governmental organization involved in incident management activities.
2. A single JIC location is preferable, but the system should be flexible and adaptable enough to accommodate multiple JIC locations when the circumstances of an incident require. Multiple JICs may be needed for a complex incident spanning a wide geographic area or multiple jurisdictions.
3. Each JIC must have procedures and protocols to communicate and coordinate effectively with other JICs, as well as with other appropriate components of the ICS organization.

JOINT INFORMATION CENTER (CONTINUED)

An example of a typical JIC organization is shown in the figure below.

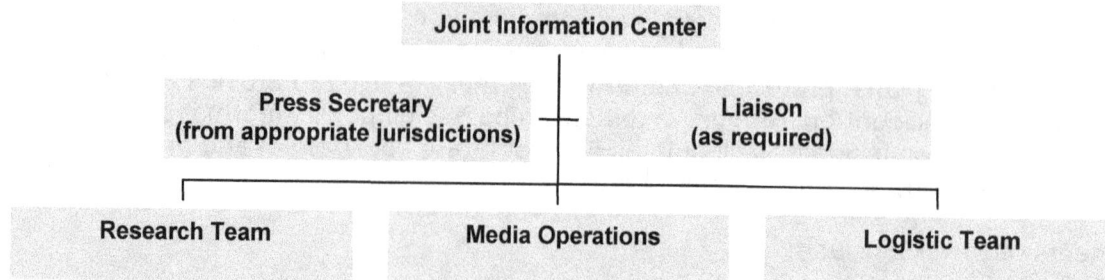

Joint Information Center Organization

A SINGLE PLANNING PROCESS AND IAP

Electing participants to work in Unified Command depends on the location and the type of event/incident. A Unified Command structure may be composed of one principal official from each jurisdiction or representatives from several responders. Because the Operations Section is the agency with greatest involvement, the Operations Section Chief usually implements the IAP. In a Unified Command, all agencies involved contribute to the command process.

Every event needs an IAP. IAPs may be written or oral, although written plans may be preferable. Either type must cover strategic goals, tactical objectives, and needed support. If an event is prolonged, it may require more than one action plan.

If the gathering is large and multiple events are taking place simultaneously, one feature of the IAP may be an event/incident timeline showing the sequence of events and their locations.

The planning process for Unified Command is similar to that used in Single Incident Command. However, one important distinction is the need in Unified Command for every jurisdictional or functional agency's Incident Commander to participate in a Command Meeting before creating the joint IAP in the first operational meeting.

This initial Command Meeting provides the responsible agency officials with an opportunity to discuss and concur on important issues before the joint IAP is created.

Command Meeting requirements include the following:

- The Command Meeting should include only agency Incident Commanders.
- The meeting should be brief, and important points should be documented.
- Prior to the meeting, the respective responsible officials should have reviewed the meeting's purposes and agenda items and be prepared to discuss them.

A Single Planning Process and IAP (Continued)

Officials attending the initial Command Meeting should:

- State their jurisdictional or agency priorities and objectives.
- Present their jurisdictional limitations, concerns, and restrictions.
- Develop a collective set of event/incident objectives.
- Establish and agree on acceptable priorities.
- Adopt a general, overall strategy or strategies to accomplish objectives.
- Agree on the basic Unified Command organizational structure.
- Designate the best-qualified and most acceptable Operations Section Chief.
- Agree on General Staff personnel designations and planning, logistical, and finance agreements and procedures.
- Agree on the resource ordering process to be followed.
- Agree on cost-sharing procedures.
- Agree on informational matters.
- Designate a single agency official to act as the Unified Command spokesperson.

Incident Action Planning meetings will use the results of the Command Meeting to determine:

- Tactical operations for the next Operational Period.
- Resource requirements and resource availability and sources.
- Resource assignments.
- The unified Operations Section organization.
- Combined Planning, Logistics, and Finance/Administration operations, as needed.

The result of the planning process will be an IAP that addresses multi-jurisdictional or multi-agency priorities and provides tactical operations and resource assignments for the unified effort.

Shared Planning, Logistics, Finance/Administration Sections

The Unified Command incident organization can also benefit by integrating multi-jurisdictional and/or multi-agency personnel into various other functional areas.

For example, in the Operations and Planning Sections, Deputy Section Chiefs can be designated from an adjacent jurisdiction which may, in future Operational Periods, have the primary responsibility for these functions.

By placing other agencies' personnel in the Planning Section's Situation, Resources, and Demobilization Units, significant savings in personnel, and increased communication and information sharing will often result.

In the Logistics Section, a Deputy Logistics Section Chief from another agency or jurisdiction can help to coordinate event/incident support as well as facilitate resource-ordering activities. Placing other agencies' personnel into the Communications Section helps in developing a single event/incidentwide Communications Plan.

SHARED PLANNING, LOGISTICS, FINANCE/ADMINISTRATION SECTIONS (CONTINUED)

Although the Finance/Administration Section often has detailed and agency-specific procedures to follow, cost savings may be realized through agreements on cost sharing for essential services. For example, one agency might provide food services, another may provide fuel, and a third may provide security.

UNIFIED COMMAND RESOURCE ORDERING

An important advantage of Unified Command over Single Incident Command is the ability of commanders to establish resource-ordering procedures before the Incident Action Planning meeting. During the Command Meeting, commanders can designate specific kinds and types of resources to be supplied by certain jurisdictions or agencies in the resource-ordering procedures. This designation depends upon the previous commitments of the responsible agency officials.

Following the Command Meeting, the Incident Action Planning meeting will determine resource requirements for all levels of the organization. The nature and location of the event/incident will, to some extent, dictate the most effective offsite resource-ordering procedure.

These resource requirements established at the Incident Action Planning meeting are given to the Logistics Section, which then creates a single resource order that is transmitted to a single agency responsible for filling the order. (Some situations may require multiple resource orders to be transmitted to multiple agencies. Multiple resource orders are generally less desirable than a single resource order, however, and they should be avoided when possible.) The agency then fills the order from the closest available resource.

Having resource-ordering procedures in place before the Incident Action Planning meeting determines the resource requirements ensures that the agency filling the resource order can do so quickly and effectively.

FUNCTIONING IN UNIFIED COMMAND

It is essential to understand how an ICS Unified Command functions. Knowledge of ICS principles of organization will enable managers to accept and easily adapt to a Unified Command mode of operation when it is required. Lack of knowledge about ICS can limit the willingness of some jurisdictions or agencies to participate in Unified Command incident organization. It is impossible to implement Unified Command unless all affected agencies have agreed to participate in the command structure.

Establishing a single Incident Command Post is essential to success. Other facilities where all agencies can operate together may be established as needed. Avoid the confusion created by separate command, planning, and logistics setups.

FUNCTIONING IN UNIFIED COMMAND (CONTINUED)

Begin action planning as early as possible after the notification of an event/incident. Initiate Unified Command as soon as two or more agencies having jurisdictional or functional responsibilities participate in, or respond to, the event or incident. Where conflicting priorities based on agency responsibilities exist, early initiation of Unified Command is especially important.

The Operations Section Chief will normally be chosen from the jurisdiction or agency that has the greatest involvement in the event/incident, although this association is not essential.

However, the Operations Section Chief should be the most qualified and most experienced person. The selection of the Operations Section Chief must be agreed upon by the Unified Command because he or she will have full authority to implement the operations portion of the IAP. The Unified Command must also agree on other General Staff personnel who will be implementing their portions of the IAP.

If necessary, the Unified Command may designate one of the ICs to act as a spokesperson. The ICs may see the need to identify one among them to act as an Operational Period Duty Officer and/or spokesperson for the Unified Command.

Designating a spokesperson can provide a channel of communications from the General and Command Staff members into the Unified Command structure. The spokesperson does not make Unified Command decisions, but does provide a point of contact as necessary for the General and Command Staffs.

Finally, it is important to conduct discussions of Unified Command with adjacent jurisdictions and functional agencies whenever possible.

Individually and collectively, the designated agency ICs functioning in a Unified Command have the following responsibilities at an event/incident:

- They must clearly understand their jurisdictional or agency limitations. Any legal, political, jurisdictional, or safety restrictions must be identified and made known to all.
- They must be authorized to perform specific activities and actions on behalf of the jurisdiction or agency they represent. These actions could include:

  - Ordering of additional resources in support of the IAP.
  - Loaning or sharing the resources of other jurisdictions.
  - Agreeing to cost-sharing arrangements with participating agencies.

FUNCTIONING IN UNIFIED COMMAND (CONTINUED)

The agencies' ICs have the responsibility to manage the event/incident to the best of their abilities. This responsibility includes:

- Working closely with the other ICs in the Unified Command.
- Providing sufficient qualified staff and resources.
- Anticipating and resolving problems.
- Delegating authority as needed.
- Inspecting and evaluating performance.
- Communicating with their own agencies to establish priorities, plans, problems, and progress.

The members of the Unified Command must function together as a team, ensuring effective coordination of the IAP. In many ways, this is the most important function they perform in Unified Command.

Manageable span of control is another aspect of ICS. Manageable span is defined as the number of subordinates one supervisor can manage effectively. Guidelines suggest from three to seven persons, with five persons being the optimum number.

The Command Post is the center for directing all operations, and only one Command Post operates during an event. Usually the IC, the Planning Section, the communications center, and all agency representatives have offices there.

PUBLIC SAFETY ROLES IN UNIFIED COMMAND

After the ICs determine a command structure, they should identify the roles of public safety personnel. They must bear in mind that all public safety organizations must also be able to answer their normal responsibilities as well as provide staffing for the event. As part of the permitting process, the promoter may be required to cover the cost for any public safety personnel responding to an event/incident.

The role of the emergency management agency is to complement and support local first responders and to coordinate and facilitate the flow of required responses to the IC as needed.

The role of Law Enforcement Agencies (EMA) may be to provide:

- Crowd management, including measures to prevent crushing.
- Control of access to stage or performance areas.
- Security control at entrances and exits.
- Patrol to minimize risk of fire.
- Control of vehicle traffic and marshaling.
- Searches for drugs, alcohol, and weapons.
- Security for large sums of money and confiscated goods.
- Assistance for emergency services, as needed.

PUBLIC SAFETY ROLES IN UNIFIED COMMAND (CONTINUED)

Depending upon jurisdiction, the role of firefighters may vary. Tasking to the fire departments and department capabilities differ for every community.

Emergency medical services may be called upon to render first aid to personnel attending the event. They may also work in cooperation with public health to provide more in-depth, onsite medical care in the form of site and field hospitals or to transport people to local medical facilities.

FEDERAL AND STATE RESOURCES

If an incident occurs that is beyond the capability of the local authorities, a community may have to request the assistance of State or Federal assets through designated State and local agencies. Event planners should be prepared to discuss the event and the locations of all of the risks with the State and Federal authorities, as needed. Providing an event footprint and grid map to State or Federal responders will help them locate areas in the event, especially if smoke or debris make locating areas difficult. Research your support and your capabilities at every level.

One way of sharing resources is through local mutual aid agreements. These agreements allow local agencies to borrow equipment and resources from neighboring communities. They also allow the lending community to be covered under the borrowing community's insurance. For example, if a community needs to borrow a pumping unit from a community three towns away and the pumping truck is damaged or is involved in an accident, the borrowing community's insurance will be responsible for damages, repairs or replacement to equipment. Sharing of resources is especially useful in smaller communities where budgets may not allow for extensive equipment.

The State and/or local Emergency Management Agency may be of assistance in locating the agency or assistance needed for a special event in the community.

CHAPTER 4: ADDITIONAL PLANNING CONSIDERATIONS FOR SPECIFIC EVENTS

INTRODUCTION

Some events present more risks than others, and they require special planning well in advance of the event. This chapter provides some examples of high-risk events and suggests ways to prepare for emergencies that may occur during those events. Planners should ensure that personnel are trained and equipped for the unique nature of these events. Another way to learn of these risks is to check with other agencies to gain additional information. For each of these high-risk events, weather is a critical factor that you must consider.

POWER BOAT RACES AND SIMILAR AQUATIC EVENTS

Before any outdoor event begins, check with the proper agencies such as the Coast Guard, natural resources, or other applicable agencies.

MEDICAL SUPPORT FOR PARTICIPANTS

Aquatic events, particularly those involving motorized watercraft, require careful planning. A designated medical response boat should be available in the water with appropriately trained personnel and equipment, including a spinal board and resuscitation equipment. The medical boat should be linked by two-way radio to the rescue boats and ambulance/medical services. For offshore boat racing, consider a helicopter with rescue capabilities.

A rescue boat should be in attendance with experienced divers, equipped with scuba gear, to remove personnel trapped underwater.

Identify landing locations appropriate for the transfer of patients on stretchers from boats to land ambulances.

SPECTATOR AREAS

Appropriate buffer walls or "run off" areas should be established to prevent out-of-control vessels from entering spectator and pit areas.

Where spectators are permitted to line piers and breakwaters along areas of deep water, observe the following practices:

- In the absence of a physical barrier, mark a line to warn spectators away from the edges fronting deep water.
- In addition to any vessel committed to assisting event participants, a dedicated boat should constantly patrol the shore adjacent to the spectator area. It should be equipped with a loudspeaker to warn spectators who venture too close to the edge. The boat should also be suitably equipped to provide for water rescue and the resuscitation of injured persons.

SPECTATOR AREAS (CONTINUED)

All boats intended for rescue, or designated to provide medical attention, should be clearly marked and equipped with some form of hazard lighting to warn other vessels off. Any boats used for participant or spectator control should be staffed with personnel trained in appropriate lifesaving and emergency medical practices, including cardiopulmonary resuscitation (CPR).

Any boat intended for medical assistance or water rescue should contain sufficient clear space to resuscitate a patient in the supine position and be equipped, at a minimum, with the following:

- Automatic External Defibrillator (AED).
- A spinal board for full-body immobilization, and cervical collars and restraint straps.
- Ventilation equipment, which should ideally be a positive pressure oxygen ventilator, or as a minimum, a bag-valve-mask unit, preferably with oxygen assist (oropharyngeal airways and suction should also be included).
- A supply of large pressure dressings.
- Personnel trained and experienced in the use of the equipment identified above.
- Personnel trained and attired to perform water rescue and removal.

AUTOMOBILE AND SIMILAR RACES

While aquatic events present hazards to participants and spectators, and difficulties to event planners and incident responders that are not present with other events, some types of auto racing also present unique areas of concern.

Sponsors of organized auto races conducted by professional racing organizations at permanent facilities normally meet the safety guidelines required for participants as outlined in this document. Similarly, professional racing organizations using temporary facilities follow very strict guidelines.

For racing events conducted by local clubs, however, no formal safety guidelines exist to cover the health and safety of participants and spectators. Motor Cross races, bicycle races, and specialized automobile rallies are a source of great concern because of both the very limited control exercised over spectators and the often-remote locations in which they are held. Spectators often position themselves in remote, almost inaccessible, areas where the action is expected to be spectacular. The entire course should be monitored as well as possible, and a suitable communications system should be in place.

MEDICAL SUPPORT FOR PARTICIPANTS

In the event of a crash, an ambulance with a trained staff should be available immediately. The medical support staff must understand the racing rules and be trained to recognize the various flags and special warning lights used by race officials. Understanding the racing rules and the signals ensures that the staff knows how soon another racing vehicle will arrive at the accident scene, whether or not the crashed vehicle remains on the track.

At smaller club events, having an ambulance on standby may be cost-prohibitive, and other suitable arrangements must be made. In such circumstances, a designated vehicle with appropriate equipment and trained personnel should be available to serve as the ambulance. The vehicle should not be merely a van with basic equipment provided as an ad hoc measure.

The standby ambulance or other emergency vehicle should be positioned for controlled, rapid access to the track. An appropriate communications system and acknowledged procedures should be in place to activate an immediate ambulance response to a track emergency, while track officials control the activity on the track with flags or other signals.

Guidelines should be established in advance to determine:

- Whether the race will continue if the ambulance leaves to transport a patient and no backup ambulance is available to take its place.
- Whether the ambulance will be designated strictly for the participants, and if so, what means are available to assist with medical emergencies among the spectators.

If possible, the race should be stopped when an ambulance or other emergency vehicle is on the track, even though some races continue to run under the caution flag.

Suitable "first attack" firefighting and rescue equipment should also be available at the track. If onsite resources are not able to respond successfully to an emergency, procedures to obtain additional rapid fire and rescue service must be in place.

If you expect great risk to participants and spectators, large numbers of spectators, or if the nearest hospital is very distant, consider providing a site hospital.

SPECTATOR AREAS

Barriers should be in place to isolate spectators from out-of-control vehicles. Experience shows, however, that these barriers can be moved or broken by out-of-control vehicles, resulting in injuries to spectators who are leaning against the barriers. Further enhance safety by posting a compulsory "no man's land" to keep spectators away from the barrier fence.

Individuals responsible for barrier design, including barrier height and strength, should take into account the possibility that one vehicle may mount another or somersault end over end. A barrier intended to retard penetration by a single impacting vehicle is insufficient.

Spectator Areas (Continued)

In addition, parts of automobiles involved in collisions can become projectiles, and wheels can come loose and bounce into spectator areas. To protect spectators, affix a strong wire-mesh debris screen to the barrier fencing and to the tops of retaining walls. The wire-mesh screen permits spectator visibility while serving as a trap for projectiles.

Carefully monitor spectator access if spectators are permitted to visit the track and pit areas at any time, including after the race. Participants often test vehicles after the event, with neither drivers nor spectators anticipating each other's presence on the track.

Major problems, including spectator injuries, have occurred at a number of events with spectators accessing the track after the winner has passed the finish line, but while other competitors are still racing. All officials should be briefed on ways to control spectators who intend to access the track and how to respond if those control measures fail.

Pit Areas

In-race refueling of cars in pit areas creates a potential for fire if fuel inadvertently contacts sufficiently heated parts of vehicles or is ignited by a spark. To counter this threat, appropriate and sufficiently large fire extinguishers, or other equipment suitable for extinguishing fire, must be available at refueling sites for use by trained personnel. Remind personnel that some racing fuels burn with an invisible flame.

The combination of vehicles entering the pit lane at high speed and the drivers' vision being obstructed by barriers increases the risk to both drivers and pit crews. Organizers should consider introducing speed limits in pit lanes and enforcing suitable penalties for transgressions by drivers. Ideally, organizers should also implement a system of notifying pit personnel when vehicles are entering the pits, such as a siren or horn.

Because spectators are generally unfamiliar with pit environments and procedures, organizers should restrict access to the pits to officials and members of the race crews. If spectators are permitted in the pit area, their movement must be properly controlled, to protect them from pit hazards, such as moving vehicles, hot engine parts, and sharp metal.

If possible, organizers should not permit spectators to cross the racetrack. If spectators are permitted to cross the track, then all spectator crossings should be restricted to designated crossing points that are strictly controlled by race officials. Officials should be equipped with an efficient communication system connected to the race control area, which can provide information about upcoming race traffic.

AIR SHOWS AND DISPLAYS

The hazards presented by air events are similar to those already discussed, with a few hazards being unique to these events.

Although air shows are usually staged in accordance with aviation rules and regulations, event organizers, emergency managers, and health personnel should take specific steps to reduce the risk of a serious incident.

ACROBATIC AREAS

Acrobatic maneuvers should not take place over built-up areas, but over fields, water, airstrips, or other uninhabited areas. Aircraft should not fly over spectator areas. Where aircraft execute a maneuver laterally (parallel to the ground) the direction of execution should be away from, or parallel to, the spectators, not toward or over them.

SAFETY

Onsite fire services should be capable of delivering fire-suppressing foam onto a crashed or burning aircraft. If the air show does not take place at an airport with foam-equipped trucks, consider alternate arrangements for their provision, because water-delivering fire apparatus are unsatisfactory.

Organizers should clearly understand the requirements of the coroner and air crash investigators and be prepared to assist them in the event of a mishap.

Contingency plans should state how personnel will interact with spectators following an incident (that is, cancel the show, retain the closest spectators as witnesses, or request home video cameras that might have recorded the incident).

PARACHUTE JUMPS

Events that feature parachute jumps should include designated landing zones that are safely away from spectators and create no obvious hazards to the jumpers. Parachutists can be blown off course and suffer injury or death as a result. Spectators can also be injured in the scramble to avoid a descending jumper.

FIREWORKS AND PYROTECHNICS

Shows involving fireworks or pyrotechnics also present specific risks. When event organizers plan public displays of fireworks, they should notify and consult with the local authorities, including police, fire, and emergency medical services prior to the event. Most pyrotechnic providers or contractors follow Occupational Safety and Health Administration (OSHA) safety standards for the placement of spectator seating and fireworks launch sites.

PLACEMENT OF LAUNCH SITE

Most major incidents involving fireworks can be avoided through careful design of the launch site.

In establishing a launch site, organizers must pay close attention to the anticipated or prevailing wind direction and strength, both of which may affect the flight path of fireworks and the area where debris will fall. In addition, when you establish site placement and design, prepare for the possibility of abandoning the display in an emergency.

Where possible, the launch site should be on water (for example, on a barge or pier), enabling personnel to abandon the site easily if an accident occurs and the pyrotechnic supply ignites.

A barrier must be erected between the crowd and the launch site to protect the crowd if fireworks tip over after ignition, resulting in a lateral, rather than vertical, projection.

Fireworks must not be projected over the heads of spectators because debris is often hot and can injure spectators if it falls into their eyes or onto their heads. Another concern is health effects caused by the smoke. Anticipate potential respiratory difficulties, especially in those spectators prone to breathing problems such as asthma and allergies.

If you launch fireworks over water, do not project them over flammable trees, bush areas, buildings, or boats.

Store unused fireworks in covered metal containers to prevent accidental ignition, either by staff or by descending hot particles from previously ignited fireworks.

Fire equipment, including fire extinguishers appropriate to the location, and trained firefighters should be immediately available at the launch site.

Personnel deploying and igniting fireworks should wear protective clothing, including face shields, helmets, and heavy gloves, in case of explosion or premature or delayed ignition.

After the event, personnel should carefully inspect the launch site and surrounding area to ensure that no incipient or rekindled fires are possible. All used fireworks should be soaked in water and removed from the site, along with any securing spikes, wires, or other potentially hazardous objects.

LASER DISPLAYS

Laser light shows are now frequently included as a form of entertainment at many special events. Prior to the laser light show, health care personnel onsite should understand the kinds of accidents that can occur and identify potential hazards when lasers are used. They also should know the kind and type of laser that will be used.

SPONTANEOUS EVENTS

Occasionally an event occurs without planning. Local emergency management and public safety agencies need to be aware that spontaneous events create the same need for emergency response contingencies as planned events and that safety plans or agreed-upon roles and responsibilities for participants will be established. Such spontaneous events present unique difficulties to public safety personnel because they offer no warning and, therefore, no time to plan.

Types of spontaneous events include those which:

- Are planned without official input or permits as a result of an oversight.
- Are planned without official input or permits on purpose.
- Result from other events, such as:

  - Planned local spinoff, such as a victory parade for a local sports team
  - Local focal point
  - Response to an "under-planned" primary event

- Are demonstrations, protests, or picketing:

  - Civil disobedience
  - Planned disorderly behavior
  - Spontaneous violence

Pre-existing mutual aid agreements, response plans, training, and resource lists will assist communities that are confronted with a spontaneous event. To develop these pre-existing response aids, the local emergency management agency may act as a catalyst to promote cooperation among local response agencies. A local emergency management agency can also fill its role in the Emergency Operations Center (EOC) if the spontaneous event is large enough to require the activation of the EOC.

Because spontaneous events are dynamic, a well-timed and appropriate response is critical to achieving safe outcomes. In many instances, however, the local or county public safety officials on duty are initially charged with all of the roles and responsibilities of managing the spontaneous event. At the same time, they are faced with other non-event incidents in the community. If communities train to respond to the various incidents associated with a spontaneous event, they can respond more effectively in times of emergency.

SPONTANEOUS EVENTS (CONTINUED)

Staffing, response, and public safety requirements for spontaneous events are the same or greater than those for a planned event of the same nature. Essential to the successful outcome of a spontaneous event is implementing ICS for an orderly and coordinated deployment of resources and personnel. Identifying a Staging Area where additional personnel and resources will be gathered is necessary. Briefing all personnel and establishing an appropriate span of control is critical to pre-deployment of personnel and resources in response to a spontaneous event. It may be necessary to establish a Situation Unit in the Planning Section to keep the Incident Commander informed of changes in the nature of the event.

Another essential element in anticipation of, and planning for, a spontaneous event is a continuing evaluation of other events, either locally or nationally, that may be catalysts for a spontaneous event in your community. Many spontaneous events occur with some level of expectation by public safety officials. The significant difference between an organized special event and a spontaneous event is that no planning time exists before a spontaneous event.

If a spontaneous event or unplanned mass gathering occurs in your community, time is critical and should not be wasted trying to determine how the event happened and who will be held responsible. After-action reports and investigations can fulfill that role. Critical time management requires that all energy be focused on response and activation of existing plans and cooperation among participating agencies.

EVENTS INVOLVING PRE-TEEN AND EARLY TEEN AUDIENCES

Concerts that attract younger audiences (for example, pre-teens and early teens) can create a number of difficulties. These spectators can become lost or separated from friends, miss scheduled return transportation, or lack sufficient funds to pay for alternate transportation.

Parents often take young spectators to such events and then have difficulty finding them at the conclusion of the event. If parents are using their cars to pick up children, traffic jams may prevent close access to the venue. Prior to entering the venue, parents and their children should identify a specific place to meet at the conclusion of the event.

One method to alleviate difficulties is to create a "Parents' Oasis" adjacent to the venue to provide parents with a waiting area during the concert. Coffee, soft drinks, snacks, and newspapers can be available to help parents pass the time while waiting for the event to conclude.

The concept of a "Parents' Oasis" is one that is particularly well-suited to concert events that parents would not want to attend and that their children would not want them to attend. The additional cost and effort devoted to providing such a facility are more than offset by the reduction in efforts needed to deal with the young audiences at the conclusion of the event.

EVENTS INVOLVING PRE-TEEN AND EARLY TEEN AUDIENCES (CONTINUED)

Information booths with access to the public address system and clearly identified event staff can assist lost children and their parents. Also consider the compounding effect of a major incident exacerbated by the problems of parents attempting to gain access to the area to reunite with their children or, in the worst-case scenario, trying to find out where their injured children have been taken.

Certain events may pose hazards and risks that are unique to their activity or audience. This chapter presented some of the particular hazards and high risks that event planners need to be aware of. These are not inclusive of all of the risks for which a response must be prepared. Careful planning and expecting the unexpected help to make the special event memorable and safe for sponsors, participants, and spectators.

CHAPTER 5: POST-EVENT ACTION

INTRODUCTION

The After-Action Report must be done in a timely manner and shared with the rest of the team. The After-Action Report focuses on both the positive and negative aspects of the event.

DEMOBILIZATION

Demobilization should be planned just as carefully as the event itself. Demobilization actually begins during the planning stages of an event and continues during the event. Planners must decide upon a logical order in which to release response agencies and other resources, and they must authorize a point of contact to release resources. The impact on the community and its resources must also be considered in the demobilization process. The Incident Commander should direct the demobilization process through the Demobilization Unit in the Planning Section.

POST-EVENT ANALYSIS MEETING

Following the event, all members of the planning team and those in charge of resources should meet to critique the event. For individuals who are unable to attend, providing a survey may be an option. The purpose of the Post-Event Analysis meeting is to allow open discussion of what went well and what could have gone better and to lay the groundwork for future events.

Prior to the meeting, planners should establish guidelines for discussion and select a facilitator for the meeting. The guidelines should emphasize that the meeting is intended to be a positive learning experience for all agencies, not a session to assign blame for problems that occurred during the event. The facilitator may come from the Emergency Management Agency or the lead agency, or planners may bring in a neutral third party that will maintain order if conflicts arise and agencies begin to find fault with one another. Problems should be discussed in generic terms as much as possible to avoid singling out specific agencies for criticism.

The lessons learned during one event can be used in planning for subsequent events. The agenda items discussed at the meeting, both successes and failures, should take the form of a report to be examined and discussed by officials later. If serious incidents occurred, such as a death or mass arrests, then writing the final report may have to wait until after litigation is completed. The facilitator is typically assigned the responsibility for documenting the meeting.

A log of checkout policy and procedures (which is created during the planning stage) ensures that everything is complete and that all agencies are satisfied with the outcome of the event. It is important to finalize one event before planning another.

POST-EVENT ANALYSIS MEETING (CONTINUED)

The Post-Event Analysis meeting is the final gathering of the event planning team before releasing response agencies, resource personnel, or volunteers. Before releasing response or resource personnel or volunteers, event planners should ensure that the responders have sufficient rest and the means to return to their home bases safely.

During this meeting, the promoter and planners should conclude any outstanding matters, such as financial obligations or matters concerning supplies and equipment. Planners and promoters should prepare a detailed statement of expenditures and outstanding bills as a part of the After-Action Report.

AFTER-ACTION REPORT

The facilitator or a representative of the Emergency Management Agency may be tasked to prepare the After-Action Report. This report is a vital document. The After-Action Report is composed following the critique meeting. The main purpose of an After-Action Report is to identify and document what worked, what did not work, and what could be improved. A useful After-Action Report should prevent the same kinds of mistakes and incidents from occurring at the next event. The report can also include any additional data, such as crowd control measures that were especially successful, that may be useful in planning similar future events. Everyone involved in the event (including volunteers) should contribute to this important document. After-Action Reports have no established formats. Most communities have a sample report to guide planners. If an incident occurred during the event, the planning team must prepare a summary sheet to show how personnel responded to the incident in case questions of legal liability arise later. After-Action Reports are also excellent ways to document events for historical or legal purposes, and to describe how crowd sizes were determined if estimations or formulas were used.

While this manual focuses mainly on planning for a special event, an After-Action Report focuses on improving the next event.

APPENDIX A: JOB AIDS

PRE-EVENT PLANNING MATRIX

Because responsibilities vary from jurisdiction to jurisdiction, certain risks or hazards are not always handled by only one agency. This matrix is designed for you to determine the risks and hazards your agency is accountable for handling and then refer to the corresponding page in the Job Aids manual. If more than one agency is tasked to respond to the risk or hazard, some overlap of responsibility may occur. One way to handle this is to place a "P" in the primary agency position and an "S" in the support agency position. The responsibilities of each agency must be discussed and decided in the planning stages, not when an incident occurs. Additional room is provided in the matrix to add agencies or risks as they may apply.

	County Agency	EMS	Emergency Management	FAA	FBI	Fire	Law Enforcement	Public Health	Public Works	State Agency	U.S. Secret Service	Utilities	Promoter/ Sponsor
Abandoned Vehicles Check page references for entire list													
Airspace Encroachment													
Assault on County Official													
Assault on Federal Official													
Assault on State Official													
Suspicious Package													
Bomb Threat													
Building Inspection													
Cancellation of Event													
Civil Disturbance w/ Demonstration													
Communications													
Credentials													

	County Agency	EMS	Emergency Management	FAA	FBI	Fire	Law Enforcement	Public Health	Public Works	State Agency	U.S. Secret Service	Utilities	Promoter/ Sponsor
Crowd Control													
Demonstrations													
Dignitary Protection													
EMS													
Environmental Hazards													
Evacuation of Area													
Fire													
First Aid Stations													
Food Handling													
Food Waste													
HazMat													
Hostage w/o Terrorism													
Human Waste													
Kidnapping													
Lost Child													
Lost and Found													
Media Relations													
Motorcades													
Parking													
Permitting													

	County Agency	EMS	Emergency Management	FAA	FBI	Fire	Law Enforcement	Public Health	Public Works	State Agency	U.S. Secret Service	Utilities	Promoter/ Sponsor
Potable Water													
Power Interruption													
Security/Governor													
Security/State Department													
Security													
Structural Collapse													
Terrorist act													
Terrorist Threat													
Ticketing													
Traffic Control													
Weather Hazards													
WMD: Chemical													
WMD: Biological													
WMD: Radiological													
WMD: Nuclear													
WMD: Explosive													

SPECIAL-EVENT PLANNING CHECKLIST

Name of Event: _____

Name of Applicant: _____

Address: _____ Phone: _____

City: _____ State: _____ Zip: _____

Name of Organization: _____

Address: _____ Phone: _____

City: _____ State: _____ Zip: _____

- For-Profit Organization

- Not-for-Profit Organization
  ID Number: _____

- Insurance for event (Attach a copy to this document.)

- Bond for event (Attach a copy of conditions.)

- Financial Responsibility for Public Services (e.g., police, fire, health, etc.)

Date(s) of Event: _____

Type of Event

- Arena sporting event
- Competitive road-race

  - Foot
  - Bicycle
  - Motor vehicle

- Convention
- Festival
- Live performance
- Music
- Non-competitive on public way
- Political rally
- Sales
- Speaker
- Other: _____

Expected attendance _____

SPECIAL-EVENT PLANNING CHECKLIST (CONTINUED)

Number of similar events previously sponsored _____ (Attach summary documents.)

Marketing

- Local
- Regional
- Multiple states
- National
- Event Web site

Public Access

- Open event
- Spectators limited to first _____ arrivals
- Tickets will be required for all events
- Tickets will be required for certain venues

Name of Location Venue: _____

- Indoor
- Outdoor
- Considered an alcohol-free event
- Advertised as an alcohol-free event
- Alcoholic beverages will be sold or served at venue
- Alcoholic beverages will be sold outside of venue

Location venue capacity: _____

Seasonal weather concerns: _____

Food Service

- None
- Multiple vendors
- Single concessionaire
- Water provided

Health and Safety Inspection

- Issued permit(s)
- Fire inspection
- Waste disposal plan

SPECIAL-EVENT PLANNING CHECKLIST (CONTINUED)

Health and Sanitation Plan

- Number of toilet facilities _____

- Number of trash facilities _____

- Disposal plan (Attach a copy to this document.)

Medical Plan (Complete and attach ICS Form 206.)

- Sponsor responsibility
- Public provided
- Medical services and facilities notified
- First Aid or rehab stations on site

Transportation Plan

- None
- Public transportation

    - Special routes
    - Extra capacity
    - Contract transportation
    - Emergency routing
    - Peak period capacity time frame

- Private transportation

Street or highway access: _____

Vehicle capacity factor: _____

Peak traffic period factor: _____

Parking Plan

Number of lots: _____

Total available spaces_____

- Public parking spaces _____

- Private parking spaces _____ (Attach private parking agreements.)

- Parking attendants _____

SPECIAL-EVENT PLANNING CHECKLIST (CONTINUED)

Traffic Patterns

- Public Works signing
- Event will require traffic flow or street closures (If checked, attach complete list.)
- Temporary traffic code or parking restrictions (If checked, attach list.)
- Traffic direction and control restrictions (If checked, attach list.)
- Tow truck service (If checked, attach agreements.)
- Abandoned and/or illegally parked vehicle recovery (If checked, attach agreements.)

Incident Action Plan

Attach ICS Forms 201, 202, 203 and 205.

Risk/hazard analysis

- Criminal response
- Fire response

    - Structure
    - At site
    - Vehicle

- Hazardous materials
- CBRNE
- Electrical hazards
- Medical emergencies

    - Food-related illnesses
    - First aid
    - Heat/cold exposures
    - Trauma
    - Overdoses

- Structure collapse
- Crowd rush
- Mass casualty
- Mass fatality
- Lost or missing persons/children
- Unattended packages
- Crowd dispersal
- Offender identification
- Public notification process (ICS Form 205 required)
- Access control
- Evacuation routes
- Evacuee assembly areas
- Shelters

SPECIAL-EVENT PLANNING CHECKLIST (CONTINUED)

Event Logistics

- Support
- Facilities
- Food Unit
- Communications
- Ground Support
- Air Support
- Medical Unit

Demobilization Plan

- Traffic or pedestrian egress from site
- Secondary transportation plan
- Sanitation removal
- Venue cleanup
- Traffic pattern normalization
- Contractual evaluation

    - Organizer commitments
    - Other public or private contracts

Debriefing

PROMOTER/SPONSOR CHECKLIST

Event Details

Name of Event: _____

Date(s) of Event: From: ___/___/___   To: ___/___/___

Event Time: Start:_____   Finish: _____

Site: _____

Site Address: _____

Promoter: _____

Event Manager:

Address: _____

Contact: Phone: _____   Fax: _____

After/Hours: _____   Cell: _____

E-Mail: _____   Pager: _____

Site preparation start date: _____/_____/_____   Site vacated date:_____/_____/_____

Brief details of function (including entertainment and main attractions):

_____

_____

_____

_____

_____

_____

PROMOTER/SPONSOR CHECKLIST (CONTINUED)

Sponsorship details (including any restrictions): _____

_____

_____

_____

What Legislative, Regulative, and Legal Issues Need to be Addressed?

State legislative/regulative requirements: _____

_____

_____

_____

Local legislative/regulative requirements: _____

_____

_____

_____

Permits required: (for example, liquor, pyrotechnics, fire, laser, food): _____

_____

_____

_____

_____

_____

Engineering approvals: _____

_____

Insurance required: _____

_____

PROMOTER/SPONSOR CHECKLIST (CONTINUED)

Reimbursement considerations for public agency involvement costs due to event:

_____

_____

_____

Site Details

NOTE: Include details such as: Indoor/outdoor, normal use, permanent structure, temporary site, multiple sites, site boundaries, temporary structures, natural features, likely hazards including weather, historic sites, environmental issues, parking arrangements, access and egress. Include facilities, such as: Water, toilets, food preparation, waste removal. (Attach diagram or site map.)

_____

_____

_____

_____

_____

Estimated total attendance: _____

Estimated age composition of audience:

0 – 12 years: _____ % of total audience

12 – 18 years: _____ % of total audience

18 – 25 years: _____ % of total audience

25 – 40 years: _____ % of total audience

40 – 55 years: _____ % of total audience

55 years and above: _____ % of total audience

PROMOTER/SPONSOR CHECKLIST (CONTINUED)

Admission will be by: _____ Pre-sold ticket _____ Free _____ Other: Please specify)

_____

Has this event been conducted previously?   YES / NO

If yes, when? _____

Where? _____

Event Manager: _____

Contact phone: _____   Fax: _____

If no, please detail the changes: _____

_____

What effects will the changes have? _____

_____

Key Stakeholders

	Name	**Phone**
State Government Dep't.(s):	_____	_____
Local Council(s):	_____	_____
	_____	_____
	_____	_____
Neighboring Councils:	_____	_____
	_____	_____
Police:	_____	_____
Ambulance Service:	_____	_____
First Aid Service:	_____	_____
Fire Service:	_____	_____

PROMOTER/SPONSOR CHECKLIST (CONTINUED)

Hospital/Medical Services: _____ _____

State Emergency Service: _____ _____

Security Personnel _____ _____

Liquor Licensing _____ _____

Local Hotel and Businesses: _____ _____

_____ _____

Transportation Authority: _____ _____

_____ _____

Neighbors: _____ _____

_____ _____

Other: _____ _____

Other: _____ _____

Time frame necessary for contact with stakeholders:

_____

_____

A full briefing of all of the above stakeholders is planned for _____ (date)

at _____ (venue).

Event Communications

During the event what form of communication systems will be available/provided/required for:

- Event management: _____

- Public address (internal): _____

- Public address (external): _____

- Emergency services: _____

- Coordination requirements: _____

PROMOTER/SPONSOR CHECKLIST (CONTINUED)

Event Promotion and Media Management

Can the promotion ticketing and publicity for the event include messages that clarify the focus of the event (for example, family fun, sporting contest, musical entertainment)?

Event Web site _____

The focus of the event is _____

The event promotion and publicity will promote:

- Safe drinking practices   YES / NO

- Don't drink and drive   YES / NO

- Intoxicated and underage persons will not be served alcohol   YES / NO

- Bags may be searched or restricted   YES / NO

- Glass containers permitted   YES / NO

- Water will be freely available   YES / NO

- Availability of "wet" and "dry" areas   YES / NO

- Location of facilities included on ticketing   YES / NO

- Health care advice included on ticketing   YES / NO

- Smoke-free environment   YES / NO

Security

Which type of security will be appropriate for the event?   _____

Who will be the appropriate security firm to be contracted?   _____

Event security would commence on ____/____/____ and conclude on ____/____/____

What will be the role of security?   _____

_____

PROMOTER/SPONSOR CHECKLIST (CONTINUED)

Have relevant police departments been contacted in relation to security?   YES / NO

If yes, what will be required of the police? _____

When will a briefing/debriefing be held involving police, security, bar staff and licensing personnel?

_____(Date before Event)   _____(Date after Event)

Will a briefing of all personnel and officials be provided regarding helping patrons with amenities and services?

Who will pay for event security costs, including overtime?

_____

Signage

What signage, including those required under the local liquor laws, will need to be developed and obtained?

_____

_____

_____

Will there be signage in languages other than English?   YES / NO

Transport

Does a transportation strategy need to be developed?   YES / NO

List the departments, councils and/or agencies that are likely to be involved in developing this strategy.

Name: _____ Organization: _____

Name: _____ Organization: _____

Name: _____ Organization: _____

Name: _____ Organization: _____

PROMOTER/SPONSOR CHECKLIST (CONTINUED)

Access and Egress for Patrons

What provisions can be made for patrons to access, move around, and leave the event venue without excessive queuing, or crushes (for example, gate control, pathways, free space)?

_____

_____

_____

_____

Will patrons be able to access toilets, food and bar areas, and entertainment sites without difficulty?   YES / NO

In an emergency, will patrons be able to leave the venue or move to other areas within the venue in reasonable safety?   YES / NO

Comments:

_____

_____

_____

_____

Access for Persons with Disability

What provisions need to be made for persons with a disability to access and move around the event venue?

_____

_____

Will persons with a disability be able to access toilets, food and bar areas, and entertainment sites without difficulty?   YES / NO

In an emergency, will persons with a disability be able to leave the venue without significantly impeding the movement of other patrons?   YES / NO

PROMOTER/SPONSOR CHECKLIST (CONTINUED)

Comments:

_____

_____

_____

_____

_____

Noise

What provisions can be made to minimise the level of noise at and around the event?

1. _____

2. _____

3. _____

4. _____

5. _____

Management of Alcohol

Are there any standard conditions of the licensing permit?   YES / NO

If YES, what are they?

_____

How will event personnel, specifically bar and security personnel, be trained and informed of the State and local statutes/ordinances and made aware of the responsibilities and penalties?

_____

_____

PROMOTER/SPONSOR CHECKLIST (CONTINUED)

What types of alcohol (for example beer, wine, and liquor) and other drinks will be available at the event?

_____

_____

In what types of containers will alcohol and other drinks be available (for example, glass, can or plastic containers)?

_____

_____

What provisions will be made for the collection of drink containers during and after the event?

_____

_____

What will be the pricing structure for alcoholic and non-alcoholic drinks?

_____

Is it anticipated that the pricing structure will discourage patrons from becoming unduly intoxicated?   YES / NO

Can the event publicity, ticketing, and signage inform patrons of the restrictions on alcohol including that alcohol will not be served to minors and intoxicated people?   YES / NO

Can some, if not all, bars be shut prior to the end of the entertainment?   YES / NO

If the event **is "Bring Your Own Bottle" BYOB**, what provisions can be made to prevent glass-related injuries, underage drinking, and excessive intoxication?

_____

_____

If the event **is not BYOB**, what provisions can be made to prevent alcohol from being brought into the venue?

_____

_____

_____

PROMOTER/SPONSOR CHECKLIST (CONTINUED)

If there are to be designated drinking areas, will they be adequate in size and number and supported by toilet facilities to cope with the expected size of the crowd?   YES / NO

Will there be dry areas for families, entertainment, and food?   YES / NO

Will the event provide the following facilities to encourage responsible drinking by patrons?

- Free drinking water   YES / NO

- Cheap non-alcoholic drinks   YES / NO

- Range of quality food   YES / NO

- Shade or cover   YES / NO

- Safe drinking information   YES / NO

- Quality entertainment   YES / NO

- "Wet" and "Dry" areas   YES / NO

Other Drug Use

Is it possible that drugs, including marijuana and amphetamines, may be available and used at this event?   YES / NO

List any drugs and related information known from previous experience:

_____

_____

_____

What provisions can be made to address this drug use?

_____

_____

_____

PROMOTER/SPONSOR CHECKLIST (CONTINUED)

Medical

What level of medical service is considered necessary, and for what duration?

_____

_____

_____

Who can provide this service? _____

What will be the cost of the service? _____

If it is not a local provider, what arrangements have been made to coordinate with the local ambulance service?

_____

_____

_____

What facilities will the medical service require (including helipad)?

_____

How can these be provided? _____

Animals

If the event involves animals, what arrangements will be necessary for their management, care, and well being?

_____

_____

_____

_____

_____

PROMOTER/SPONSOR CHECKLIST (CONTINUED)

If the event may affect animals, what arrangements will be necessary for their management, care, and well being?

_____

_____

_____

_____

_____

Briefing/Debriefing

A final briefing of stakeholders is planned for _____weeks prior to the event.

A debriefing will be conducted with all stakeholders within _____ days of the event.

APPROVING AUTHORITY CHECKLIST

Event Details

Name of Event:

Requested Date(s) of Event: From: _____/_____/_____   To:_____/_____/_____

Request Event Time: Start: _____   Finish: _____

Requested Site: _____

Site Address: _____

Promoter: _____

Event Manager: _____

Address: _____

Contact: Phone: _____   Fax: _____

After Hours: _____

Requested site preparation start date: _____/_____/_____

Suggested site vacated date: _____/_____/_____

Brief details of function (including entertainment and main attractions):

_____

_____

_____

_____

_____

APPROVING AUTHORITY CHECKLIST (CONTINUED)

Legal Requirements

Does the application:

- Comply with State and Local legislation/regulations/codes?   YES / NO

- Provide for adequate general public liability insurance?   YES / NO

- Provide for adequate liability insurance for a major incident?   YES / NO

- Need to post a bond to cover contingencies?   YES / NO

Licenses/Permits

Does the application require:

- Liquor licensing?   YES / NO

- Road closures/restrictions?   YES / NO

- Food outlet licenses?   YES / NO

- Health care licensing?   YES / NO

- Fire Inspection?   YES / NO

- Fireworks/pyrotechnics permits?   YES / NO

- Any other: _____

_____

Site

Is it appropriate for the type of event?   YES / NO

Are there multiple sites involved in the event?   YES / NO

Comment: _____

Indoor/outdoor: _____

APPROVING AUTHORITY CHECKLIST (CONTINUED)

Permanent structure or temporary site: _____

Normally used for this type of event?   YES / NO

Normally used for large crowds?   YES / NO

Topography:

_____

_____

_____

_____

Any effect on neighboring communities?   YES / NO

Suitability for camping facilities?   YES / NO

List any environmental issues (green, flora, fauna, historic site): _____

_____

List any natural features likely to be hazardous (river, dam, long grass, forest): _____

_____

Anticipated crowd number of attendees: _____

Is site large enough for expected crowd?   YES / NO

Tickets being pre-sold?   YES / NO   _____% Of Attendance

Tickets sold at the gate?   YES / NO   _____% Of Attendance

Other means of limiting crowd: _____

_____

_____

APPROVING AUTHORITY CHECKLIST (CONTINUED)

Type of crowd expected (young, old, family, unruly): _____

_____

Is water available at site?   YES / NO

Quality of water: _____

Quantity of potable water: _____

Probability of sabotage of water?   YES / NO

Comment: _____

_____

Fixed sewerage?   YES / NO

Adequate sewerage capacity?   YES / NO

Comment: _____

Other utility supplies (power, gas): _____

Will they be adequate? _____

Will emergency water supplies be required?   YES / NO

Will emergency water supplies be supplied?   YES / NO

Will emergency water supplies be available?   YES / NO

Comment: _____

_____

Will emergency electricity supplies be required?   YES / NO

Will emergency electricity supplies be supplied?   YES / NO

Will emergency electricity supplies be available?   YES / NO

APPROVING AUTHORITY CHECKLIST (CONTINUED)

Comment: _____

_____

_____

_____

Will emergency gas supplies be required?   YES / NO

Will emergency gas supplies be supplied?   YES / NO

Will emergency gas supplies be available?   YES / NO

Comment: _____

_____

_____

Emergency Services/Key Stakeholders

Has applicant consulted and gained support/approval from:

- State/Local Government Departments?   YES / NO

- If yes, list by abbreviation: _____

- Police Department?   YES / NO

- Ambulance Service?   YES / NO

- First Aid Service?   YES / NO

- Fire Department?   YES / NO

- Medical/Hospital Facilities?   YES / NO

- State Emergency Service?   YES / NO

- Transportation Authorities?   YES / NO

- Liquor Licensing Court?   YES / NO

- Neighboring Communities?   YES / NO

- Neighbors/Community Association?   YES / NO

APPROVING AUTHORITY CHECKLIST (CONTINUED)

Other: _____

_____

Other: _____

_____

Have emergency management plans been prepared?   YES / NO

Have contingency plans been prepared?   YES / NO

If NO, are they necessary?   YES / NO

If they are necessary, who will coordinate the preparation? _____

Security

Is special security being provided?   YES / NO

If YES, who is providing it? _____

If NO, is it considered necessary?   YES / NO

Is the provider licensed to provide the service?   YES / NO

Event Safety Issues

Natural

Weather (rain, wind, heat, cold): _____

Terrain (cliffs, creeks, reclaimed land): _____

Environmental

Animals, forests, pollens, pests, flora, fauna, historical: _____

_____

APPROVING AUTHORITY CHECKLIST (CONTINUED)

<u>Technological</u>

Utility lines, noise, lighting, access and egress: _____

_____

<u>Human</u>

Alcohol, hysteria, nuisance, neighbors, fire: _____

_____

<u>Event</u>

Pyrotechnics, lasers: _____

Access/Egress—Parking

Are road access and egress suitable?	YES / NO
Are road access and egress suitable in all weather?	YES / NO
Are road access and egress adequate?	YES / NO
Will special traffic control be required?	YES / NO
Is sufficient suitable off-road parking available?	YES / NO
Will emergency services have continual access and egress?	YES / NO
In the event of a major emergency, do access and egress allow for emergency services?	YES / NO

Food

See Job Aids Food Vendor Information Sheet and Catering Inspection Checklist for Food Vendors.

APPROVING AUTHORITY CHECKLIST (CONTINUED)

Toilets

What is the anticipated crowd mix of male and female attendees (by percentage)?

_____MALE   _____FEMALE

How many fixed-toilet facilities will be available?

_____MALE TOILETS

_____URINALS

_____MALE SHOWERS

_____FEMALE TOILETS

_____FEMALE SHOWERS

_____DISABLED

Will separate toilet facilities be available for food vendors?   YES / NO

Will separate toilet facilities be available for medical attendants?   YES / NO

Are there sufficient toilet facilities?   YES / NO

If NO, what additional requirements will there be?   _____MALE TOILETS

_____URINALS

_____MALE SHOWERS

_____FEMALE TOILETS

_____FEMALE SHOWERS

_____DISABLED

Will the current sewerage system cope with the extra demand?   YES / NO

APPROVING AUTHORITY CHECKLIST (CONTINUED)

If NO, what additional requirements will there be?

_____

_____

Where additional requirements are unserviced, can service trucks gain
easy access?   YES / NO

What servicing of toilets will be provided during the event?   _____

_____

_____

What, if any, plumbing maintenance will be available onsite?   _____

_____

Garbage and Water Removal

Number of garbage bins available   _____ Public Use

                                                             _____ Food Outlet Use

                                                             _____ Medical Facility Use

Type of garbage bins (including for sharps, wet, dry, hazardous):   _____

_____

_____

Program for emptying garbage bins: _____

_____

Program for removal of site garbage: _____

_____

_____

APPROVING AUTHORITY CHECKLIST (CONTINUED)

Restoration After Event

Arrangements for site cleanup: _____

_____

Arrangements for cleanup of surroundings (including access and egress roads): _____

_____

_____

Arrangements for refund of bond money, if applicable: _____

_____

Camping Areas (where applicable)

What is the proximity to property boundaries?

NORTH   yards   SOUTH   yards

EAST   yards   WEST   yards

What is the requested population density of the camp? _____ Persons per acre

What is the requested maximum population for each site?
                    maximum_____ persons per site

What separation is planned between sites?
                    minimum_____ yards between rows

What emergency access and egress will be available? _____

_____

APPROVING AUTHORITY CHECKLIST (CONTINUED)

What toilet and personal hygiene facilities will be available within campsite?

_____MALE TOILETS   _____FEMALE TOILETS

_____URINALS

_____MALE SHOWERS   _____FEMALE SHOWERS

_____DISABLED TOILETS   _____DISABLED SHOWERS

What water supply is available?   _____

Is it potable?   _____

Can you estimate whether this is sufficient?   YES / NO

Comments: _____

_____

What garbage bins are available?   _____

Can you estimate whether this is sufficient?   YES / NO

What waste disposal arrangements are being made (including wet, dry, sharps, sewage)?

_____

_____

Site Plan

Camp site plan available (including access and egress for emergency vehicles, access and egress for service vehicles, parking areas, camping areas, numbered camp sites, toilet and personal hygiene facilities, water points, trash bins, food venues, First Aid/Medical facilities, any other related facilities).

YES / NO

FOOD VENDOR INFORMATION SHEET
(one required for each vendor)

(To be provided to the local health authority)

Name of Vendor: _____

Point of Contact: _____

Business Address: _____

Business Phone: _____ Business Fax: _____

POC Phone: _____ POC Mobile: _____

POC Pager: _____

Main purpose of business: _____

Is a menu attached, indicating the full range of food to be provided?   YES / NO

Indicate which of the following foods you sell directly or will be using as ingredients:

- Milk/milk products   YES / NO

- Poultry   YES / NO

- Salads/rice dishes   YES / NO

- Egg products   YES / NO

- Fish/fish products   YES / NO

- Raw meat   YES / NO

- Ice cream   YES / NO

- Shellfish   YES / NO

- Cooked meat   YES / NO

Other (specify): _____

FOOD VENDOR INFORMATION SHEET (CONTINUED)

Type of operation:

- Stall   YES / NO

- Mobile unit   YES / NO

- Stand   YES / NO

- Tent   YES / NO

Other (specify): _____

Indicate the type of equipment to be provided/used on site:

- Refrigeration   YES / NO

- Freezer   YES / NO

- Oven   YES / NO

- Deep fryer   YES / NO

- Microwave oven   YES / NO

- Sink   YES / NO

- Wash hand basin   YES / NO

- Grill   YES / NO

Other (specify): _____

Are fire extinguishers provided at each site?   YES/ NO

What kind/type?: _____

Indicate power sources:

- LPG (propane)   YES / NO

- Electrical generator   YES / NO

Other (specify): _____

FOOD VENDOR INFORMATION SHEET (CONTINUED)

Is the food to be prepared or stored in premises other than the temporary food premises or vehicle?   YES / NO

If YES, please state the address: _____

_____

Will food be delivered to the site by a separate supplier?   YES / NO

If YES, what arrangements will be made for receipt of those goods? _____

_____

Have you or any of your staff completed a food handler hygiene course?   YES / NO

If YES, when and where: _____

_____

Vendor Point of Contact signature: _____

Date: _____

Location of vendor in event footprint _____

CATERING INSPECTION CHECKLIST FOR FOOD VENDORS

The establishment of a temporary catering facility can mean working in less-than-ideal conditions. The following checklist will provide guidance on minimum requirements for this type of event catering.

Setting Up

Food service operation is licensed or registered in accordance with State/local requirements.

YES / NO

The appropriate permit has been obtained from the State/local authority where the event is to be held.

YES / NO

The area for which the permit is valid is clear, that is, the location where the vendor can set up?

YES / NO

Staff Training

Staff are trained in food handling and food safety.

YES / NO

Staff have been instructed on machinery operation, food preparation routines and occupational health and safety matters.

YES / NO

There are clear guidelines for staff about what to do if problems occur (who to contact and appropriate contact numbers).

YES / NO

Food Handling

All food handlers carry out hand washing thoroughly and regularly, particularly:

- Before commencing work and after every break   YES / NO

- After visiting the toilet   YES / NO

- After handling raw food   YES / NO

- After using a handkerchief or tissue or touching nose, hair or mouth   YES / NO

YES / NO
- After handling trash

YES / NO
- After smoking

Correct food temperatures can be, and are, maintained.   YES / NO

CATERING INSPECTION CHECKLIST FOR FOOD VENDORS (CONTINUED)

Food is cooled rapidly under refrigeration in trays not more than 4 inches deep	YES / NO
Tongs are provided and used where possible for food handling.	YES / NO
Gloves, if used, are changed regularly.	YES / NO
Food is thoroughly cooked.	YES / NO
Food is protected from dust, insect pests, and other contaminating matter.	YES / NO
Staff wear suitable, clean clothing and have long hair tied back.	YES / NO
Food on display on counters is protected from contamination from the public by use of covers or guards.	YES / NO
Condiment area is checked and cleaned regularly.	YES / NO

Food Storage

Sufficient refrigeration space is provided to cope with peak demand.	YES / NO
Refrigerated storage temperatures can be maintained during peak loads.	YES / NO
Raw foods are stored below cooked or ready to eat foods.	YES / NO
Food containers are covered.	YES / NO
Food is stored off the floor on pallets or shelving	YES / NO
Frozen food is thawed on the bottom shelf in the refrigerator or under cold running water.	YES / NO
Dry food storage space is adequate for peak loads.	YES / NO
Dry foods are protected from dust and insect pests and rodents at all times.	YES / NO
Hot food storage is in accordance with applicable standards.	YES / NO
Cold food storage is in accordance with applicable standards.	YES / NO

CATERING INSPECTION CHECKLIST FOR FOOD VENDORS (CONTINUED)

Food Transport

Transport times are kept to a minimum.   YES / NO

Food temperatures are met at all times during transport.   YES / NO

All foods are protected from dust, pests, chemicals, and other contaminating matter.   YES / NO

Cleaning and Sanitizing

Cleaning cloths are replaced frequently.   YES / NO

Equipment and surfaces used for the preparation of raw foods are cleaned and sanitized before further use.   YES / NO

Sanitizers are appropriate for use in the food industry and are used in accordance with the manufacturers' directions.   YES / NO

Packaging and Labeling

All prepackaged foods are labeled in accordance with United States Food and Drug Administration nutritional requirements.   YES / NO

Waste Management

Waste is removed regularly from food preparation areas.   YES / NO

Putrescible (decomposable) waste removed from food preparation areas is placed in bins with tight-fitting lids.

Capacity to store sullage waste is adequate or connection to the sewer is maintained without leakage.   YES / NO

Infectious Diseases

All staff are required to report any gastrointestinal type illness to the supervisor.   YES / NO

A register of staff illness is kept by the supervisor.   YES / NO

Staff are not permitted to work while they have symptoms of gastrointestinal illness or in the acute stage of a cold or flu-like illness.   YES / NO

CATERING INSPECTION CHECKLIST FOR FOOD VENDORS (CONTINUED)

Safety

The workplace is safe, that is, there are no trip hazards, no unprotected hot zones, and no unguarded equipment.   YES / NO

Fire precautions are followed and fire safety devices are to the satisfaction of the fire authority.   YES / NO

Food handlers have contact details for all necessary personnel in case of problems occurring.   YES / NO

A list of appropriate contact details is maintained and accessible.   YES / NO

For example,

- Event organizer   YES / NO

- Environmental health officer   YES / NO

- Plumber   YES / NO

- Electrician   YES / NO

- Refrigeration mechanic   YES / NO

- Alternative refrigeration suppliers   YES / NO

UTILITIES DEPARTMENT VENUE ASSESSMENT CHECKLIST

Electrical—Ground Fault Interrupter and National Electrical Code (NEC) Standards

- Back-up generator with fuel supply
- Emergency lighting and exit signs
- Clearly marked distribution and disconnect
- Key personnel ID (photo and briefing)
- System security
- Alternate electrical sources

Alternative Fuels

- Valves and emergency shutoff
- Pilotless ignition

Isolation of Subsections of System

- Hood
- Carbon monoxide (CO) monitors
- Waste oil storage
- No interior storage of, or use of, unapproved systems

HVAC

- HVAC engineer on duty
- Reversible system?
- Back-up power for system

Telecommunications—E-911

Emergency system access (coded)
Event primary PSAP identified

Uninterruptible Power Supply (UPS)

- Adequate number of lines, with locations clearly marked
- Amplified receivers (ADA)
- System priority lines

UTILITIES DEPARTMENT VENUE ASSESSMENT CHECKLIST (CONTINUED)

Water

- Fire water system – Fire Department Connection (FDC)
- System grid established
- Potable water – locations, security, markings identified

Sanitary Sewer

- Adequacy
- Pre-event inspection
- Portable units, as needed, with servicing established
- Have formulas regarding toilets (male and female) been followed? (See Chapter 2 in this manual for toilet facility suggestions.)

PUBLIC WORKS DEPARTMENT CHECKLIST

Street/Drainage Division

- Barricades, traffic cones and jersey barriers.
- Transport water tankers as necessary.
- Assure sidewalks are clean and in safe condition.

Traffic Engineering Operations Division.

- Review the traffic event management plan submitted by the event manager.
- Coordinate with the Police Department regarding traffic flow patterns.
- Timing of signals changes to maximize traffic flow.
- Regional traffic management plan.

Animal Control Division

- Back-up program to respond to the event as necessary.

Solid Waste Management Division

- Collection of site debris.
- Sweeping of site and adjacent roadways.
- Litter control and disposal.
- Coordination with the Health Department concerning debris removal from food serving areas.

Parking Operations/Enforcement Division

- Review parking program and offer assistance.
- Coordinate with mass transportation organization regarding pick-up point parking.

Engineering Division

- Coordinate with organizations involved in the event to review the site and the layout of the various program.
- Work with the Building Inspections Division to coordinate the planning for the event.

Regional Mass Transportation Division

- Establish timely schedules for shuttles.
- Review the fees and charges for providing services.

PUBLIC WORKS DEPARTMENT CHECKLIST (CONTINUED)

Forestry/Horticulture Division

- Protect the landscaping in year-round planter areas from public damage.
- Inspect trees and large shrubbery for trimming as required to accommodate event security concerns and to ensure the public welfare of the event attendees.

Parks and Recreation Division

- Schedule personnel to support activities in the event area.
- Work with vendors in supplying the needed support for the event.
- Arrange for special events coordination with the children's area.

BUILDING DEPARTMENT VENUE ASSESSMENT CHECKLIST

Occupancy

Type: _____

Overload: _____

Seating: (quality, quantity, state of repair, fixed, and portable) _____

_____

Stairs/Ramps: _____

Handrails–size and capacity: _____

Adequate Exits

Number: _____

Capacity: _____

_____

Parking

Spaces: _____

Location: _____

Storage

Square feet: _____

Location: _____

Hazardous Materials

Use: _____

Storage: _____

Kind/type: _____

Security concerns: _____

BUILDING DEPARTMENT VENUE ASSESSMENT CHECKLIST (CONTINUED)

Auxiliary Power

Type: _____

Capacity: _____

Facility Use

Type: _____

History: _____

Building Inspection History

Date of last building inspection: _____

Date of last fire inspection: _____

Correction of violations: _____

Date of last elevator/escalator inspections: _____

Slip/trip/fall hazards present?: _____

Documentation/Monitoring

_____

HVAC Adequacy

Tons per square feet: _____

**Plan Review and Walk-Through Inspection with Fire Department Code
Enforcement Officer**

Building Suppression Systems: _____

ADA Compliance: _____

**Coordinate Security of Structurally Vulnerable Areas with Law Enforcement
Agency**

Catwalks, balconies, and stages: _____

BUILDING DEPARTMENT VENUE ASSESSMENT CHECKLIST (CONTINUED)

Building Owner Contact Information

Name: _____   Phone: _____

Address: _____

Billing Address: _____

Liability Insurance: _____

PUBLIC HEALTH DEPARTMENT VENUE ASSESSMENT CHECKLIST

Buildings and Facilities

- HVAC/Air quality
- Inspections – water, food vendors

Sanitation _____

Waste Disposal

Type: _____

When/how often: _____

Water

Quality: (potable): _____

Quantity: (potable): _____

Quantity: (non-potable): _____

Hot Water

Quality: _____

Quantity: _____

Cleaning Agents

- Types, use, quantity
- Toilets – fixed, portable, quantity, cleaning, inspection, and servicing
- Floors – nonslip, drains, and cleanup
- Cleanup – trash, sweeping, mopping, grass, and dust control

PUBLIC HEALTH DEPARTMENT VENUE ASSESSMENT CHECKLIST (CONTINUED)

Food—General

- Licenses – fixed and temporary
- Fire extinguishers

Food—Ice and Water

- Vector control

Food—Refrigeration/Storage

- Inspection – cleanliness, temperature, off the floor

Food—Cooking

- Devices – fuel, temperature, hot/cold, thermal, exhaust

Food—Handling

- Staff training (hygiene, cross contamination, etc.)

Food—Power Supplies

- Power Cord – ground fault interrupter

Food—Generators

- Fuel
- Refueling
- Exhaust
- Operators

Sneeze Shields/Covers

_____

First Aid Kits

_____

FIRE SERVICES VENUE ASSESSMENT CHECKLIST

Exit Doors

- Appropriate number
- Appropriate locations
- Appropriate size
- Appropriate operation
- Appropriate markings

Avenues of Egress

- Sufficient width
- Adequate accessibility

Exit Route Markings

- Sufficient size
- Sufficient numbers
- Understandable
- Emergency lighting

Notification Systems

- Smoke
- Heat detectors
- Pull boxes
- Fire watch
- Carbon monoxide
- On line and functioning, monitored detection systems

Automated Fire Protection

- Sprinklers
- Zones
- Grids
- Hoods

Manual Fire Protection

- Extinguishers
- Hose lines
- Connections

FIRE SERVICES VENUE ASSESSMENT CHECKLIST (CONTINUED)

Fire Department Connections

- Sprinkler: locations _____
- Standpipe: locations_____

Fire Department Response

- Time
- Size of assignment

Fire Spread Ratings of Stage Materials

_____

Pyrotechnic Safety Used in the Show

Permit obtained?   YES / NO

Licensed show provider?   YES / NO

Other?: _____

Need for On-Duty Inspector and Technical Expert for HVAC System

_____

Develop, Review and/or Update Plan for Event Site/Buildings

_____

Ensure Occupancy Load is Posted and Not Exceeded

_____

Fire Lane Marked and Kept Clear

_____

911 System Access:
Handheld radio / cellular phone / landline (NOT pay phone)

LAW ENFORCEMENT VENUE ASSESSMENT CHECKLIST

Crowd Control/Site Security

Access by the public: _____

Access by VIPs: _____

Access by emergency services: _____

Secondary route: _____

Security concerns: _____

Demographics of Spectators and Participants

Age: _____

Mobility: _____

Numbers: _____

Attitude: _____

VIP's to attend: _____

Patrols

Uniformed: _____

Non-uniformed: _____

Other security: _____

Intelligence contact: (Joint Terrorism Task Force (JTTF), etc.)

Traffic

Control: access/egress _____

Concerns: _____

LAW ENFORCEMENT VENUE ASSESSMENT CHECKLIST (CONTINUED)

Alcohol

- None
- Limited access (such as beer gardens): _____
- Distributing locations on event footprint

Incident Command Post

Location and contact information: _____

Closest mutual aid resources if required?

Promoter background investigation completed?

Surveillance: (closed-circuit television, locations, etc.)

Credentialing required?

Meals/lodging arrangements made for staff, if required?

Overtime considerations addressed?

Arrest/booking process identified?

Special teams required? (SWAT, EOD, K-9, etc.)

EMERGENCY MEDICAL SERVICES VENUE ASSESSMENT CHECKLIST

Event Type

Hazards: _____

Vulnerabilities: _____

Environment

Indoor/Outdoor: _____

Climate: _____

Alcohol/Drugs: _____

Demographics of Spectators and Participants

Age: _____

Mobility: _____

Numbers: _____

Attitude: _____

VIPs: _____

Transportation

Access/Egress: _____

Americans with Disabilities Act (ADA) Compliance: _____

_____

Internal/External: _____

Facility

Visibility/Lighting: _____

EMERGENCY MEDICAL SERVICES VENUE ASSESSMENT CHECKLIST (CONTINUED)

Fixed or Festival Seating: _____

Layout: _____

ADA Compliance: _____

Communications

Internal: _____

External: _____

Aid Station on Site   YES / NO

Number: _____

Staffed for event?   YES / NO

Mobile teams to be used   YES / NO

Foot: YES / NO   Number: _____

Bike: YES/ NO   Number: _____

Carts: YES / NO   Number: _____

Other: YES / NO   Number: _____

HAZARD VULNERABILITY ASSESSMENT

Frequency Distributions

The planning team should assign a *frequency distribution* for each type of hazard identified in the Rating Worksheet. A frequency distribution categorizes the jurisdiction's *exposure* to each hazard (that is, the likelihood of occurrence for each type of hazard). Exposure can be assessed in terms of cycles, hours, or years. The definitions of frequency distribution are shown in the table below.

Exposure	Frequency
Highly likely = 3	The potential for impact is very probable (near 100 percent) in the next year.
Likely = 2	The potential for impact is between 10 and 100 percent within the next year. or There is at least one chance of occurrence within the next 10 years.
Possible = 1	The potential for impact is between 1 and 10 percent within the next year. or There is at least one chance of occurrence within the next 100 years.
Unlikely = 0	The potential for impact is less than 1 percent in the next 100 years.

HAZARD VULNERABILITY ASSESSMENT (CONTINUED)

Severity Ratings

The planning team should use historical and analytical data to assign a *severity rating* to each type of hazard that the team identifies in the hazard rating worksheet. The severity ratings selected should quantify, to the degree possible, the damage to be expected in the jurisdiction as a result of a specific hazard. The definitions of the severity ratings are shown in the table below.

Population/Property Level of Severity	Definition
Catastrophic = 3	Multiple deaths. Complete shutdown of critical facilities for 30 days or more. More than 50 percent of property is severely damaged.
Critical = 2	Injuries and/or illnesses result in permanent disability. Complete shutdown of critical facilities for at least 2 weeks. More than 25 percent of property is severely damaged.
Limited = 1	Injuries and/or illnesses do not result in permanent disability. Complete shutdown of critical facilities for more than 1 week. More than 10 percent of property is severely damaged.
Negligible = 0	Injuries and/or illnesses are treatable with first aid. Minor quality of life lost. Shutdown of critical facilities and services for 24 hours or less. No more than 1 percent of property is severely damaged.

HAZARD VULNERABILITY ASSESSMENT (CONTINUED)

Ranking the Hazards

Using the severity and frequency distribution definitions, the planning team should identify potential hazards for the event and rank them in the Rating Worksheet.

Hazard	Frequency (Likelihood)	Potential Impact on Population	Potential Impact on Property	Level of Coverage in EOP	Point Total
	0 = Unlikely 1 = Possible 2 = Likely 3 = Highly Likely	0 = Negligible 1 = Limited 2 = Critical 3 = Catastrophic	0 = Negligible 1 = Limited 2 = Critical 3 = Catastrophic	0 = None 1 = Limited 2 = Sufficient 3 = Comprehensive (annex)	
	0 1 2 3	0 1 2 3	0 1 2 3	0 1 2 3	
	0 1 2 3	0 1 2 3	0 1 2 3	0 1 2 3	
	0 1 2 3	0 1 2 3	0 1 2 3	0 1 2 3	
	0 1 2 3	0 1 2 3	0 1 2 3	0 1 2 3	
	0 1 2 3	0 1 2 3	0 1 2 3	0 1 2 3	
	0 1 2 3	0 1 2 3	0 1 2 3	0 1 2 3	
	0 1 2 3	0 1 2 3	0 1 2 3	0 1 2 3	
	0 1 2 3	0 1 2 3	0 1 2 3	0 1 2 3	
	0 1 2 3	0 1 2 3	0 1 2 3	0 1 2 3	
	0 1 2 3	0 1 2 3	0 1 2 3	0 1 2 3	
	0 1 2 3	0 1 2 3	0 1 2 3	0 1 2 3	
	0 1 2 3	0 1 2 3	0 1 2 3	0 1 2 3	

HAZARD VULNERABILITY ASSESSMENT (CONTINUED)

Recording the Information

Using the information from the Rating Worksheet, the planning team should complete the Profile Worksheet to assess each hazard.

Hazard Profile Worksheet
Hazard_____
Potential Magnitude • Catastrophic: Can affect more than 50 percent of the jurisdiction. • Critical: Can affect between 25 and 50 percent of the jurisdiction. • Limited: Can affect between 10 and 25 percent of the jurisdiction. • Negligible: Can affect less than 10 percent of the jurisdiction.
Areas Likely to be Most Affected (by sector) _____
Probable Duration _____
Potential Speed of Onset • More than 24 hours' warning probably will be available. • Between 12 and 24 hours' warning probably will be available. • Between 6 and 12 hours' warning will be available. • Minimal (or no) warning will be available.
Existing Warning Systems _____
Complete Vulnerability Analysis with local/State emergency management agencies?*   YES/NO

* Note that some hazards may pose such a limited threat to the jurisdiction that additional analysis is not necessary.

LOST-CHILD INFORMATION SHEET
(Check local regulations for reporting and release requirements.)

Date and time of report: _____

Case number (if needed): _____ Officer assigned: _____

Date and time of assignment: _____

Resolution

- Child was found. Location: _____ By whom: _____
- Name of parent/legal guardian that child was released to:_____
- Parent left and did not return to CP after being advised to stay.
- Child was not found. Report was filed. Complaint number: _____

Information About the Child

Name: _____

Address: _____

DOB: _____ Phone number: _____

Description of Child

Height: _____ Weight: _____ Hair color: _____ Eye color: _____

Clothing: _____

Unique physical features: _____

_____

Other individuals with missing child: _____

_____

Parent/Guardian Information

Name: _____

Address: _____

Phone number: _____ DOB: _____

Social Security #: _____

Form of identification provided: _____

GASTROINTESTINAL ILLNESS QUESTIONNAIRE
(For use at medical aid posts during gatherings,
to be used in addition to any patient information intake form.)

Date: _____/_____/_____   Officer assigned: _____

Name: _____

Address: _____

Phone number: _____

What symptoms have you had?

Diarrhea   YES / NO

Nausea   YES / NO

Vomiting   YES / NO

Abdominal cramps   YES / NO

Headache   YES / NO

Fever   YES / NO

Blood in feces   YES / NO

Joint or muscle aches   YES / NO

Other: _____

When did the symptoms first start?

Date: _____/_____/_____

Time: _____ a.m./p.m.

Do you know of others who have been ill with similar symptoms?   YES / NO

(Include names and contact details for others on the reverse side of this form for further followup.)

What have you eaten since being at this event and where was it purchased or obtained?

(List the food history on the reverse side of this form. Include all food, drinks, and any other snacks. It is important to list where the food was obtained.)   YES / NO

GASTROINTESTINAL ILLNESS QUESTIONNAIRE (CONTINUED)

Have you been swimming since being at this event?

Pool	YES / NO
Spa	YES / NO
River	YES / NO
Lake	YES / NO

Other: _____

Do you suspect anything that may have caused your illness?   YES / NO

Explain: _____

_____

_____

NOTE: Keep this form for review or collection by the supervisor or public health official. Report anything suspicious or, if there are several cases, similar illness within a short period of time. Provide a report to local emergency rooms and those in surrounding communities for statistical analysis and distribution.

INCIDENT ACTION PLAN SCHEDULE

Operational Period:

Date:

	Form	Responsibility	Time Needed By
Cover			
Incident Objectives	202		
Organization Assignment	203		
Division Assignment	204		
Communication Plan	205		
Medical Plan	206		
Traffic Plan			
Weather Forecast			
Fire Behavior Forecast			
Air Operations Summary	220		
Safety Message			
Tool and Equipment Plan			
Finance Message			
Rehabilitation Plan			
Cover			

ICS FORM 201 – INCIDENT BRIEFING

Purpose: The Incident Briefing form provides the Incident Commander (and the Command and General Staffs assuming command of the incident) with basic information regarding the incident situation and the resources allocated to the incident. It also serves as a permanent record of the initial response to the incident.

Preparation: The briefing is prepared by the Incident Commander for presentation to the incoming Incident Commander along with a more detailed oral briefing. Proper symbology should be used when preparing a map of the incident.

Distribution: After the initial briefing of the Incident Commander and General Staff members, the Incident Briefing form is duplicated and distributed to the Command Staff, Section Chiefs, Branch Directors, Division/Group Supervisors, and appropriate Planning and Logistics Section Unit Leaders. The sketch map and summary of current action portions of the briefing form are given to the Situation Unit while the Current Organization and Resources Summary portion are given to the Resources Unit.

Instructions for Completing the Incident Briefing (ICS Form 201)

Item Number	Item Title	Instructions
1.	Incident Name	Print the name assigned to the incident.
2.	Date Prepared	Enter date prepared (month, day, year).
3.	Time Prepared	Enter time prepared (24-hour clock).
4.	Map Sketch	Show perimeter and control lines, resource assignments, incident facilities, and other special information on a sketch map or attached to the topographic or orthophoto map.
5.	Prepared By	Enter the name and position of the person completing the form.
	Resources Ordered	Enter the number and type of resource ordered.
	Resource Identification	Enter the agency three-letter designator, S/T, Kind/Type and resource designator.
	ETA/On Scene	Enter the estimated arrival time and place the arrival time or a checkmark in the "on the scene" column upon arrival.

ICS FORM 201 – INCIDENT BRIEFING (CONTINUED)

Item Number	Item Title	Instructions
	Location/Assignment	Enter the assigned location of the resource and/or the actual assignment.
6.	Summary of Current Actions	Enter the strategy and tactics used for the incident and note any specific problem areas.
7.	Current Organization	Enter on the organization chart the names of the individuals assigned to each position. Modify the chart as necessary.
8.	Resource Summary	Enter the following information about the resources allocated to the incident. Enter the number and type of resources ordered.
*NOTE		Additional pages may be added to ICS Form 201 if needed.

ICS FORM 201 – INCIDENT BRIEFING (CONTINUED)

Incident Briefing	1. Incident Name	2. Date Prepared	3. Time Prepared

4. Map Sketch

ICS 201	Page 1	5. Prepared by (Name and Position)

ICS Form 201 – Incident Briefing (Continued)

6. Summary of Current Actions

ICS 201	Page 2	

ICS FORM 201 – INCIDENT BRIEFING (CONTINUED)

7. Current Organization

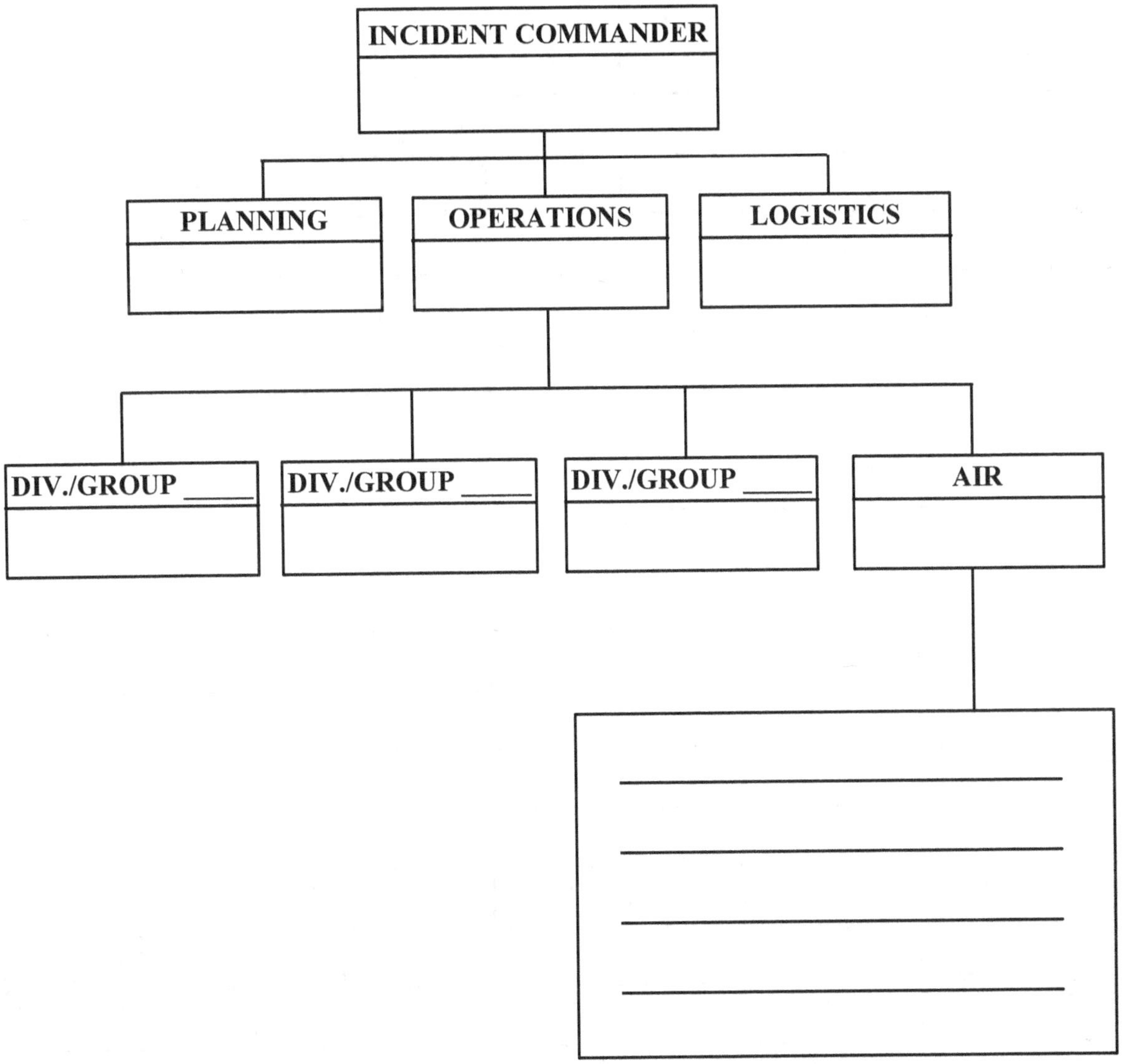

```
                    INCIDENT COMMANDER


        PLANNING         OPERATIONS         LOGISTICS


  DIV./GROUP ___   DIV./GROUP ___   DIV./GROUP ___      AIR
```

| ICS 201
(12/93)
NFES 1325 | Page 3 | |

ICS FORM 201 – INCIDENT BRIEFING (CONTINUED)

8. Resource Summary				
Resources Ordered	Resources Identification	ETA	On Scene ✓	Location/Assignment
ICS 201	Page 4			

ICS FORM 202—INCIDENT OBJECTIVES

Instructions for Completing the Incident Objectives (ICS Form 202)

Item Number	Item Title	Instructions
		NOTE: ICS Form 202, Incident Objectives, serves only as a cover sheet and is not considered complete until attachments are included.
1.	Incident Name	Print the name assigned to the incident.
2.	Date Prepared	Enter date prepared (month, day, year).
3.	Time Prepared	Enter time prepared (24-hour clock).
4.	Operational Period	Enter the time interval for which the form applies. Record the start time and end time and include date(s).
5.	General Control Objectives (Include alternatives)	Enter short, clear, and concise statements of the objectives for managing the incident, including alternatives. The control objectives usually apply for the duration of the incident.
6.	Weather Forecast for Operational Period	Enter weather prediction information for the specified operational period.
7.	General Safety Message	Enter information such as known safety hazards and specific precautions to be observed during this operational period. If available, a safety message should be referenced and attached.
8.	Attachments	The form is ready for distribution when appropriate attachments are completed and attached to the form.
9.	Prepared By	Enter the name and position of the person completing the form (usually the Planning Section Chief).
10.	Approved By	Enter the name and position of the person approving the form (usually the Incident Commander).

ICS form 202—Incident Objectives (Continued)

INCIDENT OBJECTIVES	1. Incident Name	2. Date	3. Time
4. Operational Period			
5. General Control Objectives for the Incident (include alternatives)			
6. Weather Forecast for Period			
7. General Safety Message			

8. Attachments (mark if attached)

☐ Organization List – ICS 203	☐ Medical Plan – ICS 206	☐ (Other)
☐ Div. Assignment Lists – ICS 204	☐ Incident Map	☐
☐ Communications Plan – ICS 205	☐ Traffic Plan	☐

9. Prepared by (Planning Section Chief)	10. Approved by (Incident Commander)

ICS 202

ICS FORM 203–ORGANIZATION ASSIGNMENT LIST

Purpose: The Organization Assignment List provides ICS personnel with information on the Units that are currently activated and the names of personnel staffing each position or Unit. It is used to complete the Incident Organization Chart (ICS Form 207) which is posted on the Incident Command Post display.

Preparation: The list is prepared and maintained by the Resources Unit under the direction of the Planning Section Chief.

Distribution: The Organization Assignment List is duplicated and attached to the Incident Objectives form and given to all recipients of the Incident Action Plan.

Instructions for Completing the Organization Assignment List (ICS Form 203)

Item Number	Item Title	Instructions
		An Organization Assignment List may be completed any time the number of personnel assigned to the incident increases or decreases or a change in assignment occurs.
1.	Incident Name	Print the name assigned to the incident.
2.	Date Prepared	Enter date prepared (month, day, year).
3.	Time Prepared	Enter time prepared (24-hour clock).
4.	Operational Period	Enter the time interval for which the assignment list applies. Record the start time and end time and include date(s).
5 through 10.		Enter the names of personnel staffing each of the listed positions. Use at least first initial and last name. For Units indicate Unit Leader and for Division/Groups indicate Division/Group Supervisor. Use an additional page if more than three Branches are activated.
	Prepared By	Enter the name of the Resources Unit member preparing the form. Attach form to the Incident Objectives.

ICS FORM 203–ORGANIZATION ASSIGNMENT LIST (CONTINUED)

ORGANIZATION ASSIGNMENT LIST				
1. Incident Name		Chief		
2. Date	3. Time	Deputy		
4. Operational Period		**a. Branch I – Division/Groups**		
Position	Name	Branch Director		
5. Incident Commander and Staff		Deputy		
Incident Commander		Division/Group		
Deputy		Division/Group		
Safety Officer		Division/Group		
Information		Division/Group		
Liaison Officer		Division/Group		
6. Agency Representative		**b. Branch II – Division/Groups**		
Agency	Name	Branch Director		
		Deputy		
		Division/Group		
		Division/Group		
		Division/Group		
		Division/Group		
7. Planning Section		Division/Group		
Chief		**c. Branch III – Division/Groups**		
Deputy		Branch Director		
Resources Unit		Deputy		
Situation Unit		Division/Group		
Documentation Unit		Division/Group		
Demobilization Unit		Division/Group		
Technical Specialists		Division/Group		
Human Resources		Division/Group		
Training		**d. Air Operations Branch**		
		Air Operations Branch Director		
		Air Attack Supervisor		
		Air Support Supervisor		
		Helicopter Coordinator		
8. Logistics Section		Air Tanker Coordinator		
Chief		**10. Finance/Administration Section**		
Deputy		Chief		
Supply Unit		Deputy		
Facilities Unit		Time Unit		
Ground Support Unit		Procurement Unit		
Communications Unit		Compensation/Claims Unit		
Medical Unit		Cost Unit		
Security Unit				
Food Unit		Prepared by (Resource Unit Leader)		
9. Operations Section				

ICS Form 205–Incident Radio Communications Plan

Purpose: The Incident Radio Communications Plan provides in one location information on all radio frequency assignments for each Operational Period. The plan is a summary of information obtained from the Radio Requirements Worksheet (ICS Form 216) and the Radio Frequency Assignment Worksheet (ICS Form 217). Information from the Radio Communications Plan on frequency assignments is normally placed on the appropriate Assignment List (ICS Form 204).

Preparation: The Incident Radio Communications Plan is prepared by the Communications Unit Leader and given to the Planning Section Chief. Detailed instructions on preparing this form may be found in ICS 223-5, Communications Unit Position Manual.

Distribution: The Incident Radio Communications Plan is duplicated and given to all recipients of the Incident Objectives form including the Incident Communications Center. Information from the plan is placed on Assignment Lists.

Instructions for Completing the Incident Radio Communications Plan (ICS Form 205)

Item Number	Item Title	Instructions
1.	Incident Name	Print the name assigned to the incident.
2.	Date/Time Prepared	Enter date (month, day, year) and time prepared (24-hour clock).
3.	Operational Period Date/Time	Enter the date and time interval for which the Radio Communications Plan applies. Record the start time and end time and include date(s).
4.	Basic Radio Channel Utilization System/Cache	Enter the radio cache system(s) assigned and used for the incident (e.g., Boise Cache, FIREMARS, Region 5, Emergency Cache, etc.).
	Channel	Enter the radio channel numbers assigned.
	Function	Enter the function each channel number is assigned (i.e., command, support, division, tactical, and ground-to-air.)
	Frequency	Enter the radio frequency tone number assigned to each specified function (e.g., 153.400).

ICS FORM 205–INCIDENT RADIO COMMUNICATIONS PLAN (CONTINUED)

Item Number	Item Title	Instructions
	Assignment	Enter the ICS organization assigned to each of the designated frequencies (e.g., Branch I, Division A).
	Remarks	This section should include narrative information regarding special situations.
5.	Prepared By	Enter the names of the Communications Unit Leader preparing the form.

ICS FORM 205–INCIDENT RADIO COMMUNICATIONS PLAN (CONTINUED)

INCIDENT RADIO COMMUNICATIONS PLAN	1. INCIDENT NAME	2. DATE/TIME PREPARED	3. OPERATIONAL PERIOD DATE/TIME

4. BASIC RADIO CHANNEL UTILIZATION

SYSTEM/CACHE	CHANNEL	FUNCTION	FREQUENCY	ASSIGNMENT	REMARKS

5. PREPARED BY (COMMUNICATIONS UNIT)

205   ICS   9/86

NFES 1330

ICS FORM 206—MEDICAL PLAN (CONTINUED)

Medical Plan	Incident Name:	Date Prepared:	Time Prepared:	Operational Period:

5. Incident Medical Aid Stations

Medical Aid Stations	Location	Paramedics? Yes—No	

6. Transportation
A. Ambulance Services

Name	Location	Phone Number	Paramedics? Yes—No	

B. Incident Ambulances

Name	Location	Paramedics? Yes—No	

7. Hospitals

Name	Address	Travel Time		Phone Number	Helipad		Burn Center	
		Air	Ground		Yes	No	Yes	No

8. Medical Emergency Procedures

ICS 206

ICS FORM 207—INCIDENT ORGANIZATION CHART

Purpose: The Incident Organization Chart is used to indicate what ICS organizational elements are currently activated and the names of personnel staffing each element. The attached chart is an example of the kind of organizational chart used in ICS. Personnel responsible for managing organizational positions would be listed in each box, as appropriate.

Preparation: The organization chart is prepared by the Resources Unit and posted along with other displays at the Incident Command Post. A chart is completed for each Operational Period and updated when organizational changes occur.

Distribution: When completed, the chart is posted on the display board located at the Incident Command Post.

Wall-Size Chart: The ICS 207 WS is a large chart that can be posted on the command post display board for better visibility.

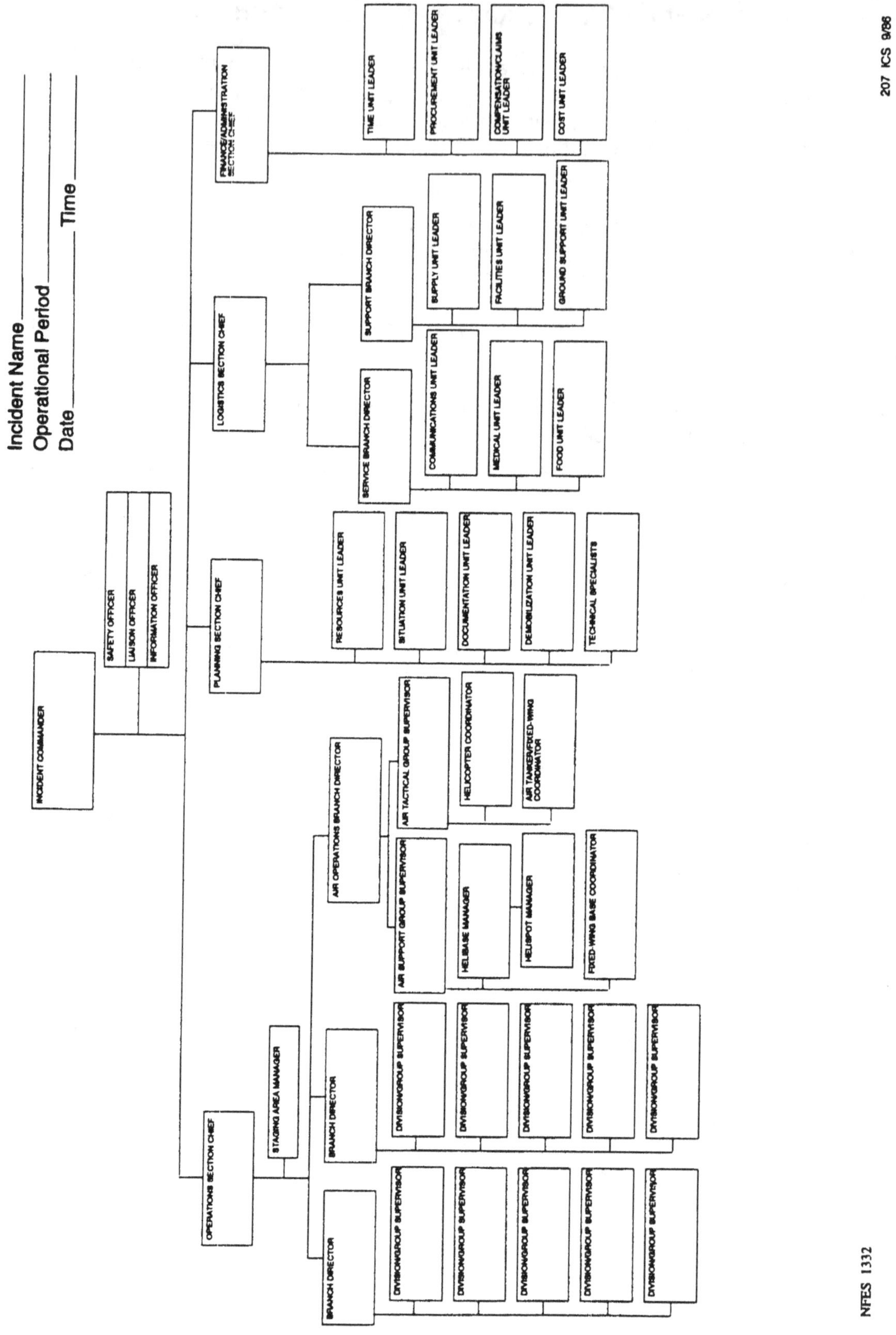

The following is an organizational chart with the following boxes:

Incident Name _____
Operational Period _____
Date _____ **Time** _____

INCIDENT COMMANDER
- SAFETY OFFICER
- LIAISON OFFICER
- INFORMATION OFFICER

OPERATIONS SECTION CHIEF
- STAGING AREA MANAGER
- BRANCH DIRECTOR
  - DIVISION/GROUP SUPERVISOR
  - DIVISION/GROUP SUPERVISOR
  - DIVISION/GROUP SUPERVISOR
  - DIVISION/GROUP SUPERVISOR
  - DIVISION/GROUP SUPERVISOR
- BRANCH DIRECTOR
  - DIVISION/GROUP SUPERVISOR
  - DIVISION/GROUP SUPERVISOR
  - DIVISION/GROUP SUPERVISOR
  - DIVISION/GROUP SUPERVISOR
  - DIVISION/GROUP SUPERVISOR
- AIR OPERATIONS BRANCH DIRECTOR
  - AIR SUPPORT GROUP SUPERVISOR
    - HELIBASE MANAGER
    - HELISPOT MANAGER
    - FIXED-WING BASE COORDINATOR
  - AIR TACTICAL GROUP SUPERVISOR
    - HELICOPTER COORDINATOR
    - AIR TANKER/FIXED-WING COORDINATOR

PLANNING SECTION CHIEF
- RESOURCES UNIT LEADER
- SITUATION UNIT LEADER
- DOCUMENTATION UNIT LEADER
- DEMOBILIZATION UNIT LEADER
- TECHNICAL SPECIALISTS

LOGISTICS SECTION CHIEF
- SERVICE BRANCH DIRECTOR
  - COMMUNICATIONS UNIT LEADER
  - MEDICAL UNIT LEADER
  - FOOD UNIT LEADER
- SUPPORT BRANCH DIRECTOR
  - SUPPLY UNIT LEADER
  - FACILITIES UNIT LEADER
  - GROUND SUPPORT UNIT LEADER

FINANCE/ADMINISTRATION SECTION CHIEF
- TIME UNIT LEADER
- PROCUREMENT UNIT LEADER
- COMPENSATION/CLAIMS UNIT LEADER
- COST UNIT LEADER

207 ICS 9/86

NFES 1332

ICS FORM 213—GENERAL MESSAGE

GENERAL MESSAGE		
TO:	POSITION	
FROM	POSITION	
SUBJECT		DATE	TIME

MESSAGE:

| |
| |
| |
| |
| |
| |
| |
| |
| |

SIGNATURE/POSITION

REPLY

| |
| |
| |
| |
| |
| |

DATE	TIME	SIGNATURE/POSITION

| 213 | ICS 1-79 | **SENDER:** REMOVE THIS COPY, FOR YOUR FILE |

PERSON RECEIVING GENERAL MESSAGE KEEP THIS COPY

RETURN THIS COPY TO SENDER

ICS FORM 214—UNIT LOG

UNIT LOG	INCIDENT NAME	DATE PREPARED
UNIT NAME	UNIT LEADER	OPERATIONAL PERIOD

ACTIVITY LOG

TIME	MAJOR EVENTS
	7. PREPARED BY (NAME AND POSITION)

ICS 214

EXPENSE REPORT

Prepared by:
Date / time:
Incident:
Name: Title: SS#:

DATE:							TOTAL
LOCATION:							
T I M E	Regular Hours						
	Overtime Hours						
T R A N S P O R T A T I O N	Vehicle Mileage						
	Common Carrier Transportation Cost						
	Vehicle Fuel/Oil Cost						
	Tolls						
	Vehicle Repair Cost						
O T H E R	Lodging Cost						
	Meals Cost						
	Equipment Repair Cost						
	Miscellaneous						
EXPENSE TOTAL							

NOTE: Attach copies of travel vouchers, meal receipts, hotel bills, lodging requests, toll receipts, and/or repair bills. Copy of time sheet and copy of vehicle cost record and gas or repair receipts must be submitted prior to, or as part of, the demobilization process.

HazMat/CBRNE Data Collection Report

Reported by: _____

Phone Number: _____

Agency or Home Address: _____

Date and Time of Incident: _____

Incident Location and Description

Neighborhood and occupancy: _____

Topography: Urban Rural Suburban

Describe: _____

Population sensitive areas (for example, nursing homes, schools, or hospitals):

Reason for Report

- Unusual liquid droplets
- Unusual odors
- Unusual cloud or vapor
- Unusual metal debris

- People becoming sick
- People dying
- Dead/discolored vegetation
- Dead/dying or sick animals

- Other (describe): _____

Weather

- Clear
- Misty
- Temperature: _____
- Relative humidity: _____

- Cloudy
- Rain
- Snow

- Other (describe): _____

HazMat/CBRNE Data Collection Report (Continued)

Wind

Direction (to/from): _____

Speed (none, mild, gusts, high winds): _____

Other (describe): _____

Odor

- None
- Irritating
- Garlic/Horseradish
- Sweet
- Pepper
- Fruity
- Changing
- Other (describe): _____

- Flower
- Forest
- Almond/Peach
- Fresh hay
- Rotten eggs

Visible Emission

- Cloud or Vapor
- Mist
- Smoke
- Liquid
- Other (describe): _____

Signs and Symptoms

- None
- Tightness in chest
- Dizziness
- Blurred vision
- Difficulty breathing
- Fever
- Runny nose
- Other (describe): _____

- Stinging of skin
- Reddening of skin
- Welts/Blisters
- Nausea/Vomiting
- Choking
- Diarrhea

HazMat/CBRNE Data Collection Report (Continued)

Date and Time of Onset: _____

Duration of Symptom(s): _____

Number of Casualties: _____

Explosion/Fires

- None
- Air
- Ground
- Other (describe): _____

- Structure
- Underground

Describe device: _____

Describe container/condition/size: _____

Describe location where device was found: _____

Describe structures involved/estimated damage: _____

Report filed by:

Information reported to: _____

BOMB THREAT CHECKLIST

Place by each telephone. Duplicate as necessary.

Exact date and time of call: _____

Exact words of caller: _____

_____

Questions to ask

1. When is the bomb going to explode? _____

2. Where is the bomb? _____

3. What does it look like? _____

4. What kind of bomb is it? _____

5. What will cause it to explode? _____

6. Did you place the bomb? _____

7. Why? _____

8. Where are you calling from? _____

9. What is your address? _____

10. What is your name? _____

Caller's Voice (Please circle appropriate terms.)

calm	disguised	nasal	angry	broken
stutter	slow	sincere	lisp	rapid
giggling	deep	crying	squeaky	excited
stressed	accent	loud	slurred	normal

If voice is familiar, whom did it sound like? _____

Were there any background noises? _____

Remarks: _____

Person receiving call: _____

Telephone number where call was received: _____

Report call immediately to: _____
(Refer to bomb incident plan.)

BOMB THREAT STAND-OFF

THREAT	THREAT DESCRIPTION	EXPLOSIVE CAPACITY	LETHAL AIRBLAST RANGE	MANDATORY EVACUATION DISTANCE	DESIRED EVACUATION DISTANCE
	Pipe Bomb	5 LBS / 2.3 KG	25 FT / 8 M	70 FT / 21 M	850 FT / 259 M
	Briefcase or Suitcase Bomb	50 LBS / 23 KG	40 FT / 12 M	150 FT / 46 M	1,850 FT / 564 M
	Compact Sedan	220 LBS / 100 KG	60 FT / 18 M	240 FT / 73 M	915 FT / 279 M
	Sedan	500 LBS / 227 KG	100 FT / 30 M	320 FT / 98 M	1,050 FT / 320 M
	Van	1,000 LBS / 454 KG	125 FT / 38 M	400 FT / 122 M	1,200 FT / 366 M
	Moving Van or Delivery Truck	4,000LBS / 1,814KG	200 FT / 61 M	640 FT / 195 M	1,750 FT / 534 M
	Semi-Trailer	40,000 LBS / 18,144 KG	450FT / 137M	1,400FT / 427M	3,500FT / 1,607M

Explosive Capacity is based on maximum volume or weight of explosives (TNT equivalent) that could reasonably fit or be hidden in a suitcase or vehicle.

Lethal Airblast Range is the minimum distance personnel in the open are expected to survive blast effects. This minimum range is based on anticipation of avoiding severe lung damage or fatal impact injury from body translation.

Mandatory Evacuation Distance is the range within which all buildings must be evacuated. From this range outward to the Desired Evacuation Distance, personnel may remain inside buildings but away from windows and exterior walls. Evacuated personnel must move to the Desired Evacuation Distance.

APPENDIX B: REFERENCES AND BIBLIOGRAPHY

REFERENCES AND BIBLIOGRAPHY

American College of Emergency Physicians Publications. <u>Provision of Emergency Medical Care for Crowds</u>. American College of Emergency Physicians Publications, 1989-90.

Australian and New Zealand Food Standards Authority. <u>Food Standards Code</u>. Canberra: Australian Government Publishing Service, Australian and New Zealand Food Standards Authority, 1987.

Australian National Health and Medical Research Council. <u>Australian Guidelines for Recreational Use of Water</u>. Canberra: Australian Government Publishing Service, National Health and Medical Research Council, 1990.

Australian Uniform Building Regulations Coordinating Council. <u>Building Code of Australia</u>. Australia: Australian Uniform Building Regulations Coordinating Council, 1990.

Barbera, J. A., et al. "Urban Search and Rescue." <u>Emergency Medicine Clinics of North America</u> May 1996.

Berlonghi, Alexander E. "Understanding and Planning for Different Spectator Crowds." <u>Engineering for Crowd Safety</u>. Ed. R.A. Smith and J.F. Dickie. Elsevier Science Publications B.V., 1993.

Billie, P., et al. "Public Health at the 1984 Summer Olympics: The Los Angeles County Experience." <u>American Journal of Public Health</u> June 1988.

Bock, H. C., et al. <u>Demographics of Emergency medical Care at the Indianapolis 500 Mile Race (1983 - 1990)</u> October 1992.

Canadian Government. <u>Aid of the Civil Power: Chapter N, Sections 274-285</u>, in <u>Revised Statutes of Canada</u>. Canada: Canadian Government, 1985.

Chapman, K.R., et al. "Medical Services for Outdoor Rock Music Festivals." <u>CMA Journal</u> 15 April 1982: 935-938.

City of Fremantle. <u>Concerts in Fremantle</u>. Western Australia: City of Fremantle, 1996.

City of Keene. "Special Event Planning Checklist." New Hampshire: City of Keene.

"Controlling the Rock Festival Crowd." <u>Security World</u> June 1980: 40-43.
    http://www.crowdsafe.com

Curry, Jack. <u>Woodstock—The Summer of Our Lives</u>. New York: Weidenfeld & Nicolson, 1989.

Defense Threat Reduction Agency. <u>Weapons of Mass Destruction Handbook</u>. Washington: Defense Threat Reduction Agency, 1 July 1999.

REFERENCES AND BIBLIOGRAPHY (CONTINUED)

Department of the Treasury: Bureau of Alcohol, Tobacco and Firearms. "ATF Vehicle Bomb Explosion Hazard and Evacuation Distance Tables." Washington, 22 Dec. 1999. <http://www.atf.treas.gov/pub/154001.htm>.

Donald, Ian. "Crowd Behavior at the King's Cross Underground Disaster." Easingwold Papers No. 4: Lessons Learned from Crowd-Related Disasters. Yorkshire: Emergency Planning College, 1992.

Emergency Management Australia. Australian Emergency Management Manual—Disaster Medicine. Australia: Emergency Management Australia, 1995. (Second edition due 1999.)

Emergency Management Australia. Australian Emergency Manual—Disaster Recovery. Australia: Emergency Management Australia, 1996. (Second edition due 2000.)

Emergency Management Australia. Australian Emergency Manuals Series: Part III, Volume 1, Manual 1—Emergency Catering. Australia: Emergency Management Australia, 1998.

Emergency Management Australia. Australian Emergency Manuals Series: Part III, Volume 2, Manual 1—Evacuation Planning. Australia: Emergency Management Australia, 1998.

Emergency Management Australia. Australian Emergency Manuals Series: Part III, Volume 2, Manual 2—Safe and Healthy Mass Gatherings. Australia: Emergency Management Australia, 1998.

Emergency Management Australia. Australian Emergency Manuals Series: Part III, Volume 3, Manual 1—Multi-Agency Incident Management. Australia: Emergency Management Australia, 1998.

Emergency Management Australia. Australian Emergency Manuals Series: Part III, Volume 3, Manual 2—Community and Personal Support Services. Australia: Emergency Management Australia, 1998.

Emergency Management Australia. Australian Emergency Manuals Series: Part IV, Manual 2—Operations Centre Management. Australia: Emergency Management Australia, 1996.

Emergency Management Australia. Australian Emergency Manuals Series: Part IV, Manual 9—Communications. Australia: Emergency Management Australia. 2nd ed. 1998.

"Emergency Medicine: Rock and Other Mass Medical." Emergency Medicine. June 1975: 116-129.

REFERENCES AND BIBLIOGRAPHY (CONTINUED)

Federal Emergency Management Agency, Emergency Management Institute. The Emergency Planning Process: Self Instruction. Emmitsburg, Maryland: Federal Emergency Management Agency, June 1997.

Federal Emergency Management Agency, Emergency Management Institute. Tools for Emergency Planning. Emmitsburg, Maryland: Federal Emergency Management Agency, Emergency Management Institute, June 1997.

Federal Emergency Management Agency, National Fire Academy. Emergency Medical Services: Special Operations. Emmitsburg, Maryland: Federal Emergency Management Agency.

Franaszek, J. "Medical Care at Mass Gatherings." Annals of Emergency Medicine May 1986: 148-149.

Fruin, John J. "Causes and Prevention of Crowd Disasters." Student Activities Programming. Oct. 1981: 48-53.

Goldaber, Irving. "Is Spectator Violence Inevitable?" Auditorium News April 1979: 4-7.

Great Britain Health and Safety Commission, Home Office and the Scottish Office. "Guide to Health, Safety and Welfare at Pop Concerts and Similar Events." London: Great Britain Health and Safety Commission, Home Office and the Scottish Office, 1993.

Hanna, James A. Emergency Preparedness Guidelines for Mass, Crowd-Intensive Events. Canada: Emergency Preparedness Canada, 1995.

---. "Rock and Peace Festivals—The Field Hospital." Disaster Planning for Health Care Facilities. 3rd ed. Ottawa: Canadian Hospital Association, 1995. 247-256.

---. "Special Events Management—Health, Safety and Emergency Planning." Lecture notes. Humber College, Toronto, 1989.

Health Department of Western Australia. "Operational Guidelines for Rave Parties, Concerts, and Large Public Events." Western Australia: Health Department of Western Australia, 1995.

Herman, Gary. Rock 'N' Roll Babylon. London: Plexus Publishing, 1982.

Hillmore, Peter. Live Aid. Parsippany, N.J.: Unicorn Publishing, 1985.

"Hillsborough: Inquiry Highlighted Differing Approach to Operational Messages." Fire. Great Britain, Aug. 1989: 7-8.

"Hillsborough: An Earlier Call Would Probably Not Have Saved Lives." Fire. Great Britain, Sept. 1989: 7.

REFERENCES AND BIBLIOGRAPHY (CONTINUED)

Hopkins, Jerry. Festival. New York: Macmillan, 1970.

International Association of Assembly Managers

James, S.H., et al. "Medical and Toxicological Aspects of the Watkins Glen Rock Concert." Journal of Forensic Sciences, n.d. (circa 1974): 71-82.

Leonard, R.B. "Medical Support for Mass Gatherings." Emergency Medicine Clinics of North America May 1996.

Lewis, J. M. "A Protocol for the Comparative Analysis of Sports Crowd Violence." International Journal of Mass Emergencies and Disaster 1988: 221-225.

Lewis, J.M. "Theories of the Crowd: Some Cross-Cultural Perspectives." Easingwold Papers No. 4: Lessons Learned from Crowd-Related Disasters. Yorkshire: Emergency Planning College, 1992.

Lichtenstein, Irwin. "EMS at Rock Concerts." Fire Chief Magazine Nov. 1983: 44-46.

Mariano, J. P. "First Aid for Live Aid." JEMS Feb. 1986.

Miami-Dade County Office of Emergency Management. Concept of Operations Plan, SuperBowl XXXIII. Florida: Miami-Dade County Office of Emergency Management. Jan. 1999.

National Domestic Preparedness Office. "WMD Threats: Sample Guidelines Reissue." Special Bulletin. Washington: National Domestic Preparedness Office, 12 Jan 2000.

National Interagency Fire Center. "ICS Glossary." In Incident Command System National Training Curriculum. Boise, Idaho: National Interagency Fire Center, Oct. 1994.

National Interagency Fire Center. "ICS Position Descriptions and Responsibilities." In Incident Command System National Training Curriculum. Boise, Idaho: National Interagency Fire Center, Oct. 1994.

National Interagency Fire Center. "Organizing for Incidents or Events, Module 8." In Incident Command System National Training Curriculum. Boise, Idaho: National Interagency Fire Center, Oct. 1994.

Ounanian, L. L. "Medical Care at the 1982 U.S. Festival." Annals of Emergency Medicine May 1986: 25-32.

Parrillo, S.J. "Medical Care at Mass Gatherings: Considerations for Physician Involvement." Prehospital and Disaster Medicine Oct.-Dec. 1995.

REFERENCES AND BIBLIOGRAPHY (CONTINUED)

Parrillo, S. J. "EMS and Mass Gatherings"
        <http://www.emedicine.com/emerg/topics812.htm>. 16 Nov. 1999.

Pauls, J.L. Observations of Crowd Conditions at Rock Concert in Exhibition Stadium.
        Ottawa: National Research Council of Canada, April 1982.

Pennsylvania Emergency Management Agency. "First Responder's Guide: Terrorism
        Incidents." Pennsylvania Emergency Management Agency.
        <http://www.state.pa.us/PA_Exec/PEMA/ema/plans/terguide.htm>. 7 Jan. 2000.

Public Entity Risk Institute - <www.riskinstitute.org>

Queensland Police Service: Drug and Alcohol Co-ordination. Alcohol, Safety and Event
        Management: A Resource to Assist Event Managers to Conduct Safer Public Events.
        Queensland: Queensland Police Service, 1997.

Rosenman, Joel, et al. Young Men With Unlimited Capital. New York: Harcourt 1974.

Ryan, S., and M. Carey. "Key Principles in Ensuring Crowd Safety in Public Venues."
        Engineering for Crowd Safety. Ed. R. A. Smith and J. A. Dickie. Elsevier Science
        Publications, 1993.

Sanders, Arthur B., et al. "An Analysis of Medical Care at Mass Gatherings." Annals of
        Emergency Medicine May 1986: 17-21.

Schlight, Judith, et al. "Medical Aspects of Large Outdoor Festivals." The Lancet 29 April
        1972: 948-952.

Taylor, Derek. It Was Twenty Years Ago Today. New York: Simon & Schuster, 1987.

Thompson, James M., et al. "Level of Medical Care Required for Mass Gatherings." Annals
        of Emergency Medicine April 1991: 78-83.

Threats: Critical Infrastructure, Key Assets – from the Department of Homeland Security,
        Buffer Zone Planning Program

"Unified Command: Module 13." Incident Command System National Training Curriculum.
        National Interagency Fir Center. Boise, Idaho. Oct. 1994.

Wardrope, J., et al. "The Hillsborough Tragedy." British Medical Journal. Nov. 1991.

Weiner, Rex, et al. Woodstock Census. New York: Fawcett Columbine, 1979.

REFERENCES AND BIBLIOGRAPHY (CONTINUED)

Wertheimer, Paul L. Crowd Management - Report of the Task Force on Crowd Control and Safety. Cincinnati: City of Cincinnati, July 1980.

Whitehead, J. "Crowd Control Can Be Critical In Emergencies." Emergency Preparedness Digest Oct.-Dec. 1989: 12-15.

Wyllie, R. " Setting the Scene" Easingwold Papers No. 4: Lessons Learned from Crowd-Related Disasters. Yorkshire: Emergency Planning College, 1992.

APPENDIX C: GLOSSARY OF TERMS

GLOSSARY

A

Action Plan	See Incident Action Plan.
ADA	Americans With Disabilities Act.
Administrative/Finance Section	The section responsible for all incident costs and financial considerations. Includes the Time Unit, Procurement Unit, Compensation/Claims Unit, and Cost Unit.
Agency	A division of government with a specific function or a non-governmental organization that offers a particular kind of assistance. In the Incident Command System (ICS), agencies are defined as jurisdictional (having statutory responsibility for incident mitigation) or assisting and/or cooperating (providing resources and/or assistance). (See Assisting Agency, Cooperating Agency, and Multi-agency.)
Agency Executive or Administrator	Chief Executive Officer of the agency or jurisdiction that has responsibility for managing the incident.
After-Action Report	A report detailing an event with recommendations for improvements.
Agency Dispatch	The agency or jurisdictional facility from which resources are allocated to incidents.
Agency Representative	An individual assigned to an incident from an assisting or cooperating agency who has been delegated full authority to make decisions on all matters affecting that agency's participation at the incident. Agency Representatives report to the Incident Liaison Officer.
Air Operations Branch Director	The person primarily responsible for preparing and implementing the air operations portion of the Incident Action Plan (IAP). Also responsible for providing logistical support to helicopters operating at the incident.
Allocated Resources	Resources dispatched to an incident.
Area Command	An organization established to 1) oversee the management of multiple incidents that are each being handled by an Incident Command System (ICS) organization; or 2) oversee the management of a very large incident that has multiple Incident Management Teams assigned to it. Area Command has the responsibility to set overall strategy and priorities, allocate assigned resources based on priorities, ensure that incidents are properly managed, and ensure that objectives are met and strategies followed.

GLOSSARY (CONTINUED)

Assigned Resources Resources checked in and assigned work tasks on an incident.

Assignments Tasks given to resources to perform within a given operational period, based upon tactical objectives in the Incident Action Plan (IAP).

Assistant Title for subordinates of the Command Staff positions. The title indicates a level of technical capability, qualifications, and responsibility subordinate to the primary positions. Assistants may also be used at other positions in the ICS organization.

Assisting Agency An agency directly contributing tactical or service resources to another agency.

Available Resources Incident-based resources that are available for assignment within 3 minutes.

B

Base The location at which primary logistics functions for an incident are coordinated and administered. There is only one base per incident. (An incident name or other designator will be added to the term *base*.) The Incident Command Post may be collocated with the base.

Branch The organizational level having functional or geographic responsibility for major parts of incident operations. The Branch level is organizationally between Section and Division/Group. Branches are identified by the use of Roman numerals.

GLOSSARY (CONTINUED)

C

Cache	A predetermined complement of tools, equipment, or supplies stored in a designated location and available for incident use.
Camp	A geographical site within the general incident area but separate from the Incident Base, and equipped and staffed to provide sleeping, food, water, and sanitary services to incident personnel.
Check-in	The process whereby resources first report to an incident. Check-in locations are as follows: Incident Command Post (Resources Unit), Incident Base, Camps, Staging Areas, Helibases, Helispots, and Division Supervisors (for direct line assignments).
Chain of Command	A series of management positions in order of authority; see Unity of Command.
Chief	The ICS title for individuals responsible for command of functional sections: Operations, Planning, Logistics, and Administration/Finance.
Clear Text	The use of plain English in radio communications transmissions. No Ten Codes or agency-specific codes are allowed when using Clear Text.
CBRNE	Chemical, Biological, Radiological, Nuclear, Explosive
Command	The act of directing or controlling resources by virtue of explicit legal, agency, or delegated authority. May also refer to the Incident Commander.
Command Staff	Consists of the Information Officer, Safety Officer, and Liaison Officer. They report directly to the Incident Commander. They may have an assistant or assistants, as needed.
Communications Unit (Comm. Unit)	An organizational unit in the Logistics Section responsible for providing communication services at an incident. A Communications Unit may also be a facility (for example, a trailer or mobile van) used to provide the major part of an Incident Communications Center.

GLOSSARY (CONTINUED)

Compensation Unit/ Claims Unit
Functional unit within the Administration/Finance Section responsible for financial concerns resulting from injuries or fatalities at the incident.

Complex
Two or more individual incidents that are located in the same general area and are assigned to a single Incident Commander or Unified Command.

Contingency Plan
A documented scheme of assigned responsibilities, actions, and procedures to be followed if an emergency situation develops.

Cooperating Agency
An agency supplying assistance other than direct tactical or support functions or resources to the incident control effort (for example, the Red Cross or telephone company).

Coordination Center
Term used to describe any facility that is used for the coordination of agency or jurisdictional resources in support of one or more incidents.

Cost Unit
Functional unit within the Administration/Finance Section responsible for tracking costs, analyzing cost data, making cost estimates, and recommending cost-saving measures.

Credential
A letter or other testimonial attesting the bearer's right to confidence or authority.

Credible Threat
A threat with sufficient credibility that would cause the FBI to begin a threat assessment. The FBI would notify law enforcement authorities within the affected State and the appropriate Federal agencies of a significant threat of terrorism.

Critical Crowd Densities
A common characteristic of crowd disasters. Critical crowd densities are approached when the floor space per standing person is reduced to about 4-5 square feet.

Crush Load
Overwhelming the capacity of a given area that results in gridlock, limited access, and hazards incompatible to life safety. This may apply to both inside and outside venues and parking areas.

Cues
A signal, hint, or guide.

GLOSSARY (CONTINUED)

D

Debrief
A meeting held during or at the end of an operation with the purpose of assessing the conduct or results of an operation.

Deputy
A fully qualified individual who, in the absence of a superior, could be delegated the authority to manage a functional operation or perform a specific task. In some cases, a Deputy could act as relief for a superior and therefore must be fully qualified in the position. Deputies can be assigned to the Incident Commander, General Staff heads, and Branch Directors.

Demobilization Unit
Functional unit within the Planning Section responsible for ensuring orderly, safe, and efficient demobilization of incident resources.

Director
The ICS title for individuals responsible for command of a Branch.

Dispatch
The implementation of a *command* decision to move a resource or resources from one place to another.

Dispatch Center
A facility from which resources are directly assigned to an incident.

Division
Divisions are used to divide an incident into geographical areas of operation. A Division is located within the ICS organization between the Task Force/Strike Team and the Branch. (See also *Group*.) Divisions are identified by alphabetic characters for horizontal applications and, often, by floor numbers when used in buildings.

Documentation Unit
Functional unit within the Planning Section responsible for collecting, recording, and safeguarding all documents relevant to the incident.

GLOSSARY (CONTINUED)

E

Emergency Medical Technician (EMT)
A healthcare professional with special skills and knowledge in pre-hospital emergency medicine.

Emergency Operating Center (EOC)
A designated facility established by an agency or jurisdiction to coordinate the overall agency or jurisdictional response and support to an emergency.

Emergency Management
A range of measures to manage risks to communities and the environment.

Emergency Management Coordinator
Refers to the individual within each political subdivision who has coordination responsibility for jurisdictional emergency management.

Emergency Management Plan
A formal record of agreed emergency management roles, responsibilities, strategies, systems, and arrangements.

Emergency Operations Plan (EOP)
The plan that each jurisdiction has and maintains for responding appropriately to hazards.

Endemic
Constant presence of a disease or infectious agent within a given geographic area or population group.

Environmental Health Officer
Terminology used that includes Health Inspectors/Surveyors, Public Health Officers, Sanitary Inspectors/Engineers, Hygiene Officers, and Preventive Health Officers.

Event
In this curriculum, an event is a planned, non-emergency activity. ICS should be used as the management system for a wide range of events (for example, parades, concerts, or sporting events).

Event Footprint
The area impacted by the event. This includes the event site(s) and any surrounding area impacted.

GLOSSARY (CONTINUED)

F

Facilities Unit	Functional unit within the Support Branch of the Logistics Section that provides fixed facilities for the incident. These facilities may include the Incident Base, feeding areas, sleeping areas, or sanitary facilities.
Field Operations Guide	A pocketsize instruction manual on the application of the Incident Command System.
Food Unit	Functional unit within the Service Branch of the Logistics Section responsible for providing meals for incident personnel.
Freelance	Term used to describe resources performing assignments on their own and not under direct ICS supervision.
Function	Term often used in reference to the five major activities in the ICS (that is, Command, Operations, Planning, Logistics, and Administration/Finance). The term *function* is used when describing the activity involved (for example, the planning function).

G

Gastric Illness (Gastroenteritis)	An inflammation of the stomach and the intestinal tract, often described as food poisoning.
General Staff	The group of incident management personnel reporting to the Incident Commander. They may each have a deputy, as needed. The General Staff consists of an Operations Section Chief, Planning Section Chief, Logistics Section Chief, and Administration/Finance Section Chief.
Goal	The end toward which incident efforts are directed.
Ground Support Unit	Functional unit within the Support Branch of the Logistics Section responsible for the fueling, maintaining, and repairing of vehicles, and for the transportation of personnel and supplies.
Group	Groups are established to divide the incident into functional areas of operation. Groups are composed of resources assembled to perform a special function not necessarily within a single geographic division. (See <u>Group</u>, under *Division*, above.)

GLOSSARY (CONTINUED)

H

Hazard Analysis	Identifies potential hazards, estimates how serious they are, and establishes planning priorities. Provides a factual basis for planning and the necessary documentation for planning and response efforts.
Helibase	The main location for parking, fueling, maintenance, and loading of helicopters operating in support of an incident. It is usually located at or near the Incident Base.
Helibase Crew	A crew of individuals who may be assigned to support helicopter operations.
Helispot	Any designated location where a helicopter can safely take off and land. Some helispots may be used for loading of supplies, equipment, or personnel.
HIPAA	Health Insurance Portability and Accountability Act.

I

Incident	An occurrence caused either by humans or by natural phenomena that requires action by emergency service personnel to prevent or minimize loss of life or damage to property and/or natural resources.
Incident Action Plan (IAP)	Contains objectives reflecting the overall incident strategy and specific tactical actions and supporting information for the next Operational Period. The plan may be oral or written. When written, the plan may have a number of forms as attachments (for example, traffic plan, safety plan, communications plan, or map).
Incident Base	Location at the incident where the primary logistics functions are coordinated and administered. (An Incident name or other designator will be added to the term *base*.) The Incident Command Post may be collocated with the Base. There is only one Base per incident.
Incident Commander (IC)	The individual responsible for the management of all incident operations at the incident site.
Incident Command Post (ICP)	The location at which the primary command function is executed. The ICP may be collocated with the incident Base or other incident facilities.

GLOSSARY (CONTINUED)

Incident Command System (ICS) The combination of facilities, equipment, personnel, procedures, and communications operating with a common organizational structure, with responsibility for the management of assigned resources to effectively accomplish stated objectives pertaining to an incident.

Incident Communication Center The location of the Communications Unit and the Message Center.

Incident Management Team The Incident Commander and appropriate General and Command Staff personnel assigned to an incident.

Incident Objectives Incident objectives provide the needed guidance and direction necessary for the selection of appropriate strategy(s) and for the tactical direction of resources. Incident objectives are based on realistic expectations of what can be accomplished when all allocated resources have been effectively deployed. Incident objectives must be achievable and measurable, yet broad enough to allow for strategic and tactical alternatives.

Incident of National Significance Incidents that require U.S. Department of Homeland Security operational and/or resource coordination. Includes: terrorism, major disasters or emergencies, and other unique situations.

Information Officer A member of the Command Staff responsible for communicating with the media or other appropriate agencies requiring information directly from the incident. There is only one Information Officer per incident.

Initial Action Resources initially committed to an incident.

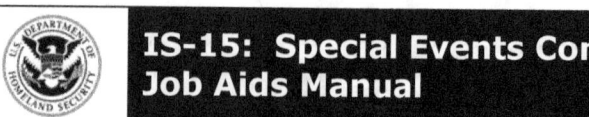
GLOSSARY (CONTINUED)

J

JIC Joint Information Center—location for coordinated media briefings.

Jurisdiction Refers to the range or sphere of authority. Public agencies have jurisdiction at an incident related to their legal responsibilities and authority for incident mitigation. Jurisdictional authority at an incident can be political/geographical (for example, city, county, State, or Federal boundary lines) or functional (for example, police department or health department). (See *Multi-jurisdiction*, below.)

Jurisdictional Agency The agency having jurisdiction and responsibility for a specific geographical area or for a mandated function.

L

Leader The ICS title for individuals responsible for a Task Force, Strike Team, or functional unit.

Liaison Officer A member of the Command Staff responsible for interacting with representatives from cooperating and assisting agencies.

Logistics Section The section responsible for providing facilities, services, and materials for the incident.

Life-Safety Highest incident priority refers to the joint consideration of both the life and physical well-being of individuals.

Life Safety Code NFPA publication- add definition

GLOSSARY (CONTINUED)

M

Managers	Individuals within ICS organizational units who are assigned specific responsibilities (for example, Staging Area Manager or Camp Manager).
Management by Objectives	In ICS, this is a top-down management activity that involves a three-step process to achieve the incident goal. The steps include establishing the incident objectives, selecting appropriate strategy(s) to achieve the objectives, and taking the tactical direction associated with the selected strategy. Tactical direction includes selecting tactics, selecting resources, assigning resources, and monitoring performance.
Mass Gathering Medicine	The management of the health and medical requirements of mass gatherings.
Medical Unit	The functional unit within the Service Branch of the Logistics Section responsible for the development of the Medical Emergency Plan and for providing emergency medical treatment of incident personnel.
Message Center	Part of the Incident Communications Center and collocated with or placed adjacent to it. It receives, records, and routes information about resources reporting to the incident, resource status, and administration and tactical traffic.
Metering	Term applied to the control procedures used to prevent critical crowd densities from developing in specific areas.
Mobilization	The process and procedures used by all organizations—Federal, State, and local—for activating, assembling, and transporting all resources that have been requested to respond to or support an incident.
Mobilization Center	An off-incident location at which emergency service personnel and equipment are temporarily located pending assignment, release, or reassignment.
Moshing	A practice carried out at concerts in which a person is supported by the upheld arms of a crowd of people. This practice is carried out in the moshpit area where the crowd is the densest.
Multi-agency Incident	An incident in which one or more agencies assist a jurisdictional agency or agencies. May be single or unified command.

GLOSSARY (CONTINUED)

Multi-agency Coordination (MAC)	A generalized term that describes the functions and activities of representatives of involved agencies or jurisdictions who come together to make decisions regarding the prioritizing of incidents and the sharing and use of critical resources. The MAC organization is *not* a part of the ICS and is *not* involved in developing incident strategy or tactics.
Multi-agency Coordination System (MACS)	The combination of personnel, facilities, equipment, procedures, and communications integrated into a common system. When activated, MACS enables the coordination of assisting agency resources and support in a multi-agency or multi-jurisdictional environment. A MAC Group functions within the MACS.
Multi-jurisdiction Incident	An incident requiring action from multiple agencies that have a statutory responsibility for incident mitigation. In ICS, these incidents should be managed under Unified Command.
Mutual Agreement	Written agreement between agencies or jurisdictions in which they agree to assist one another upon request, by furnishing personnel and equipment in an emergency situation.

N

NIMS	National Incident Management System
NRP	National Response Plan

O

Officer	The ICS title for the personnel responsible for the Command Staff positions of Safety, Liaison, and Information.
Operational Period	The period of time scheduled for execution of a given set of operation actions as specified in the Incident Action Plan. Operational Periods can be of various lengths, although usually not over 24 hours.
Operations Section	The section responsible for all tactical operations at the incident. Includes Branches, Divisions or Groups, Task Forces, Strike Teams, and Single Resources.
Out-of-Service Resources	Resources assigned to an incident but unable to respond for mechanical, rest, or personnel reasons.

GLOSSARY (CONTINUED)

P

Planning Meeting
A meeting held as needed throughout the duration of an incident to select specific strategies and tactics for incident control operations and for service and support planning. On larger incidents, the planning meeting is a major element in the development of the Incident Action Plan.

Post-Event Analysis
The final gathering of the event planning team before releasing response agencies, resource personnel, or volunteers.

Potable Water
Water that is safe for human consumption.

Procurement Unit
Functional unit within the Administration/Finance Section responsible for financial matters involving vendor contracts.

Putrescible
Waste that will decompose, such as food waste.

R

Radio Cache
A radio cache may consist of a number of portable radios, a base station and, in some cases, a repeater, all stored in a pre-determined location for dispatch to incidents.

Rave
An all-day/night dance party, especially one where techno, house, or other electronically synthesized music is played.

Recorders
Individuals within ICS organizational units who are responsible for recording information. Recorders work in Planning, Logistics, and Administration/Finance Sections.

Reinforced Response
Those resources requested in addition to the initial response.

Reporting Locations
Locations or facilities where incoming resources can check in at the incident. Refers to staging.

Resource Status Unit
Functional unit within the Planning Section responsible for recording the status of resources committed to the incident and for evaluating resources currently committed to the incident, the impact that additional responding resources will have on the incident, and anticipated resource needs.

Resource Gap Analysis
In pre-event planning the analysis of what public safety recourses the event will require versus what is locally available.

GLOSSARY (CONTINUED)

Resources
All personnel and major items of equipment available, or potentially available, for assignment to incidents. Resources are described by kind and type (for example, ground, water, and air).

Reticulated
Distribution or collection network for drinking water or sewage.

Risk Analysis
Assesses the probability of injury or damage due to a hazard and estimates the actual damage that may occur.

Risk Assessment
The process used to determine risk management priorities by evaluating and comparing the level of risk against pre-determined standards, target risk levels, or other criteria.

S

Safety Officer
A member of the Command Staff responsible for monitoring and assessing safety hazards or unsafe situations and for developing measures for ensuring personnel safety.

Sanitation
Measures taken for the promotion of public health.

Section
That organizational level with responsibility for a major functional area of the incident (for example, Operations, Planning, Logistics, Administration/Finance). The Section is organizationally located between Branch and Incident Commander.

Sector
Term used in some applications to describe an organizational level similar to an ICS Division or Group. Sector is not a part of ICS terminology.

Segment
A geographical area in which a Task Force/Strike Team Leader or supervisor of a single resource is assigned authority and responsibility for the coordination of resources and implementation of planned tactics. A segment may be a portion of a Division or an area inside or outside the perimeter of an incident. Segments are identified with Arabic numbers.

Service Branch
A Branch within the Logistics Section responsible for service activities at the incident. Includes the Communications, Medical, and Food Units.

Sewage
Waste matter that passes through sewers.

GLOSSARY (CONTINUED)

Single Resource
A piece of equipment and personnel complement, or a crew of individuals with an identified work supervisor, that can be used in a tactical application on an incident.

Situation Status Unit
The functional unit within the Planning Section responsible for the collection and organization of incident status information and for analysis of the situation as it progresses. Reports to the Planning Section Chief.

Slam Dancing
A spontaneous form of dancing where people deliberately throw themselves against people they are dancing with.

Span of Control
The supervisory ratio of from three to seven individuals, with five-to-one being established as optimal for control.

Staging Area
A temporary on-incident location where incident personnel and equipment are assigned on a 3-minute available status. Staging Areas are managed by the Operations Section.

Strategy
The general plan or direction selected to accomplish incident objectives.

Strike Team
Specified combinations of the same kind and type of resources, with common communications and a leader.

Sullage
Waste water from sinks, showers, and hand-washing basins.

Supervisor
The ICS title for individuals responsible for command of a Division or Group.

Supply Unit
Functional unit within the Support Branch of the Logistics Section responsible for ordering equipment and supplies required for incident operations.

Support Branch
A Branch within the Logistics Section responsible for providing personnel, equipment, and supplies to support incident operations. Includes the Supply, Facilities, and Group Support Units.

Support Materials
Refers to the attachments that may be included with an Incident Action Plan (for example, communications plan, map, safety plan, traffic plan, and medical plan).

GLOSSARY (CONTINUED)

T

Tactical Direction
The term includes the tactics appropriate for the selected strategy, the selection and assignment of resources, and performance monitoring for each operational period.

Target Hardening
Activities undertaken to reduce vulnerability of a venue site, i.e., installation of jersey barriers, pre-screening of attendees, etc.

Task Force
Any combination of single resources within the span of control that is assembled for a particular tactical need and has common communications and a leader.

Technical Specialists
Personnel with special skills who are activated only when needed. Technical Specialists can be used anywhere within the ICS organization.

Temporary Flight Restrictions (TFRs)
Federal Aviation Regulation 91.137 provides for the establishment of temporary airspace restrictions for non-emergency aircraft. TFRs can be requested for incidents and/or events generating a high degree of public interest, and are normally limited to a 5-nautical-mile radius and 2,000 feet above the surface.

Time Unit
Functional unit within the Administration/Finance Section responsible for recording time for incident personnel.

Topography
Physical features of place or locality.

Type
The type of any kind of resource refers to its capability compared to another type. Type 1 provides a greater overall capability due to power, size, or capacity than a Type 2 resource. Assigning type provides resource managers with additional information in selecting the best resource for the task.

GLOSSARY (CONTINUED)

U

Unified Command

In ICS, Unified Command is a unified team effort that allows all agencies with responsibility for the incident, either geographical or functional, to manage an incident by establishing a common set of incident objectives and strategies. This is accomplished without losing or abdicating agency authority, responsibility, or accountability. An Operations Section Chief is responsible for implementing the Incident Action Plan.

Unit

The organizational element having functional responsibility for a specific incident planning, logistics, or administration/finance activity.

Unity of Command

Each person within an organization reports to one designated person.

V

VBIED

Vehicle-borne improvised explosive device.

Vulnerability

The degree of susceptibility and resilience of the community and environment to hazards.

W

WMD

Weapon(s) of Mass Destruction.